Reading Andrew Fuller

H&E Readers forthcoming

Reading Jonathan Edwards
Reading the Cappadocians
Reading Augustine
Reading John Calvin
Reading John Owen

"Andrew Fuller was one of the most important Baptist theologians, evangelical theologians, and theologians of missions in all of church history. He was also one of the most important conduits of the thought of Jonathan Edwards to Great Britain. He should be more widely known and, more importantly, widely read—and this handy anthology is a great place to start. May God use these spiritual writings to inspire greater fervor for the gospel and its proclamation in the world today."

—**Douglas A. Sweeney**, Dean and Professor of Divinity,
Beeson Divinity School, Samford University, Birmingham, AL

"Significant theologians from the past cast long shadows across the landscape of ecclesiastical time thanks to reprints of their major works. The most important Christian thinkers enjoy a wider reading thanks to anthologies of selected works that expose the contemporary reader to their broader corpus. Until recently Andrew Fuller's works were available in limited ways. One could buy the classic three-volume set drawn from the nineteenth century eight-volume collection of his works or labor through a difficult to read one-volume compilation. Otherwise, the reader was limited to the much-appreciated scholarly publications of his works that are only now coming off the press. Now, thanks to this present book, faithful readers can at last experience the brilliance of Andrew Fuller's mind in an easily digestible format. The man Charles Spurgeon once lauded as 'the greatest theologian of his century' will once again bless another generation of Christians as they peruse his writings and begin to plumb the depths of his mind. I commend this work to anyone who wants to understand the Baptist way and enjoy the spiritual blessings that come with thinking about God more deeply."

—**Peter Beck**, Professor of Christian Studies,
Charleston Southern University, Charleston, SC

"Andrew Fuller has been increasingly recognised as one of the most significant and influential pastor-theologians of the English Particular Baptists in the eighteenth and early nineteenth centuries. This set of readings illustrate why he has been viewed in this light. His biblical knowledge, combined with clear theological convictions, is applied so effectively in different pastoral and missional settings. This book is warmly commended."

—**Brian Talbot**, Minister, Broughty Ferry Baptist Church and Dept of Theology, North-West University, South Africa

"Reading a work by Andrew Fuller is like water to a thirsty soul; but reading Fuller's *Works* in their entirety can be like drinking water from a fire hydrant. Michael Haykin has provided a brief but precious resource to give a 'taste' of Fuller without overwhelming us with too many words. The selection of writings is judicious and the readings themselves are delicious; each reading is preceded by a thoughtful introduction and concluded with thought-provoking questions. This is a fine resource for small group study in the church or classroom."

—**Anthony Chute**, Professor of Church History,
California Baptist University, Riverside, CA

"No one knows more about Andrew Fuller and has done more to advance Fuller scholarship than Michael Haykin. This study guide is a stellar contribution in making Fuller accessible to a wider audience. Haykin has judicially selected from among Fuller's articles, sermons, and letters and, then, framed them with trenchant introductions and probing questions that can be used equally well in church small groups and academic classrooms. It will aid readers to mine the depths and insights of one of the finest minds in the evangelical tradition."

—**Chris Chun**, Director of Jonathan Edwards Center and Professor of Church History, Gateway Seminary, Ontario, CA

"For many years, I have returned to Andrew Fuller as a personal mentor, pastor, and even friend. His keen biblical insights, pastoral sensitivity, and ardent desire to exalt Christ have refreshed my heart again and again. Fuller's impact upon the life of the church and theological scholarship is incalculable and will only be measured in eternity. This sampling of Fuller's sermons and writings from Michael A.G. Haykin will serve the church at large and perhaps even introduce Fuller to those who may be intimidated to dive into his larger works. Refresh your soul often by diving into the soul-satisfying waters of the heart and mind of Andrew Fuller as he points you toward Christ."

—**Dustin W. Benge**, Provost and Professor of Church History,
Union School of Theology, Bridgend, Wales

READING ANDREW FULLER

Michael A.G. Haykin

H&E
Academic

Reading Andrew Fuller

Copyright © Michael A.G. Haykin 2020
All rights reserved. This book or any portion thereof may not be reproduced or used in any manner whatsoever without the express written permission of the publisher except for the use of brief quotations in a book review.

Published by: H&E Publishing, Peterborough, Ontario
www.hesedandemet.com

Cover design by Chance Faulkner
Cover image Andrew Fuller by Marcos Rodrigues, 2020
Colourization of cover image by Paul Cox www.reftoons.com

Paperback ISBN: 978-1-989174-68-5
EBook ISBN: 978-1-989174-69-2

To
Jared and Anna Leigh Skinner,
for the joy of their friendship &
for the blessing they have been
to myself and my family

Contents

Introduction 1

1. Confession of Faith 7
2. An Enquiry into the Causes of Declension in Religion 17
3. The Qualifications and Encouragement of a Faithful Minister 35
4. On Liberty 59
5. On the Doctrine of Universal Salvation 73
6. Why Christians in the Present Day Possess Less Joy 81
7. The Practical Uses of Christian Baptism 97
8. To the Christian Females of Great Britain 113
9. Christian Patriotism 121
10. An Essay on Truth 139
11. The Promise of the Spirit 159
12. On Being Missional 173

Scripture Index 183

Introduction

Michael A.G. Haykin

When my classes at the Southern Baptist Theological Seminary and at Heritage College and Seminary in Cambridge, Ontario, moved online during the 2020 pandemic, I developed a deeper appreciation for the value of online theological education. Fuelling that appreciation was the creation of a webinar that I led and that was based around the reading of select works of the Baptist pastor-theologian Andrew Fuller (1754–1815), one of Christianity's great theologians. Twice a week during the months of June and July in the summer of 2020, ten or so of us met online for an hour at a time to discuss and reflect on Fuller's thinking as reflected in these texts. All of the texts that we discussed are included in this reader along with a selection from Fuller's reply to the doctrine of Universalism from 1793 and an extraordinary letter on being missional that Fuller wrote in 1811.

The goal of this small volume is to guide someone who has read little or none of Fuller through key elements of his thinking. In order to include complete pieces—articles, a sermon, and letters—I have purposely chosen not to include extracts from any of his major polemical works, with one exception, Fuller's response to Universalism. In one other case, Fuller's *Essay on Truth*, I have included only half of the text, rather than the whole piece, and this for the sake of space. This essay neatly breaks into two parts and the selection included could easily be a stand-alone piece.

Following each selection there is a series of questions. These could form the backbone of a typical academic course of study over thirteen weeks (assuming that the first week would provide an overview of Fuller's life and times), or they could be used for personal study, or, as I employed them, as the heart of a group study. They are arranged chronologically.

Who was Andrew Fuller?
Andrew Fuller was born in Wicken, a small agricultural village in Cambridgeshire.[1] His working-class parents Robert Fuller (1723–1781) and Philippa Gunton (1726–1816), were farmers who rented a succession of dairy farms. In 1761 his parents moved a short distance to Soham, where he and his family began to regularly attend the local Particular Baptist church, and where Fuller was converted in November, 1769. After being baptized the following spring, he became a member of the Soham church. In 1774 Fuller was called to the pastorate of this work. He stayed until 1782, when he became the pastor of the Particular Baptist congregation at Kettering, where he ministered till his death in 1815.

His time as a pastor in Soham was a decisive period for the shaping of Fuller's theological perspective. It was during this period that he began a life-long study of the works of the American divine Jonathan Edwards (1703–1758), who has been rightly called "America's Augustine."[2] Along with Fuller's ardent desire to live under the authority of the infallible Scriptures,[3] his reading of Edwards enabled

---

[1] For Fuller's life, the classic study is that of John Ryland, *The Work of Faith, the Labour of Love, and the Patience of Hope Illustrated; in the Life and Death of the Reverend Andrew Fuller* (London: Button & Son, 1816). A second edition of this biography appeared in 1818.
For more recent studies, see especially Gilbert S. Laws, *Andrew Fuller: Pastor, Theologian, Ropeholder* (London: Carey Press, 1942); E.F. Clipsham, "Andrew Fuller and Fullerism: A Study in Evangelical Calvinism," *The Baptist Quarterly* 20 (1963–1964): 99–114, 146–154, 214–225, 268–276; Paul Brewster, *Andrew Fuller: Model Pastor-Theologian* (Nashville, TN: B&H Academic, 2010); Peter J. Morden, *The Life and Thought of Andrew Fuller (1754–1815)* (Milton Keynes, England: Paternoster, 2015); and John Piper, Andrew Fuller: *Holy Faith, Worthy Gospel, World Mission* (Wheaton, IL: Crossway, 2016).

[2] Advertisement for "Global Jonathan Edwards Congress" (www.jedcon.be; accessed August 8, 2020).

[3] For example, Fuller could state: "If any man venerate the authority of Scripture, he must receive it as being what it professes to be, and for all the purposes for which it professes to be written. If the Scriptures profess to be divinely inspired, and assume to be the infallible

INTRODUCTION

him to become what his close friend John Ryland, Jr. (1753–1825) described as "perhaps the most judicious and able theological writer that ever belonged to our denomination,"[4] that is, the English Particular Baptists. Fuller not only provided substantial responses to major eighteenth-century heterodoxies such as Hyper-Calvinism, Deism, Socinianism, Universalism, Antinomianism, and Sandemanianism, but he also provided the theological ballast for the fledgling modern missionary movement that has led to the globalization of Christianity in the past century. Indeed, Fuller's theology, known while he was still alive as "Fullerism," powerfully "demonstrated that a man can be both a Calvinist and an Evangelical."[5]

Subsequent generations have confirmed Ryland's estimation of his friend. The Victorian Baptist preacher, C.H. Spurgeon (1834–1892), for instance, once described Fuller as the "greatest theologian" of his century, while more recently, British historian David Bebbington has stated that he is increasingly conscious of Fuller's "extraordinary importance in the history of theology."[6]

Further reading

If you wish to read more about Fuller, his thought and his times, the best place to begin would be one or two of the biographies listed in footnote 1 above. For an overview of the era in which he lived and the larger Particular Baptist community, see Raymond Brown, *The*

---

standard of faith and practice, we must either receive them as such, or, if we would be consistent, disown the writers as imposters" (*The Calvinistic and Socinian Systems Examined and Compared, as to their Moral Tendency* in *The Complete Works of the Rev. Andrew Fuller*, ed. Joseph Belcher [1845, Harrisonburg, VA: Sprinkle Publications, 1988], *Works*, II, 196).

[4] *The Indwelling and Righteousness of Christ no Security against Corporeal Death, but the Source of Spiritual and Eternal Life* (London, 1815), 2-3.

[5] Arthur H. Kirkby, "Andrew Fuller—Evangelical Calvinist," *The Baptist Quarterly* 15 (1953–1954): 195.

[6] Laws, *Andrew Fuller*, 127; David Bebbington, e-mail to author, March 11, 2009. In point of fact, there is every good reason to view Spurgeon's ministry as part of Fuller's legacy. See Steve Weaver, "C.H. Spurgeon: A Fullerite?," *Journal of Baptist Studies* 8 (February 2016): 99-117.

English Baptists of the Eighteenth Century (London: The Baptist Historical Society, 1986). For a study of some of Fuller's close friends, see Michael A.G. Haykin, *One heart and one soul: John Sutcliff of Olney, his friends, and his times* (Darlington, Co. Durham: Evangelical Press, 1994).[7] For his thinking about the church and ministry, especially see Keith S. Grant, *Andrew Fuller and the Evangelical Renewal of Pastoral Theology*, Studies in Baptist History and Thought, vol. 36 (Milton Keynes, England: Paternoster, 2013).

As I noted, I have not included any selections from Fuller's polemical works apart from the Vidler item. Understandably, these have been the focus of most of the scholarship on Fuller. See, for example, Michael A.G. Haykin, ed. *'At the Pure Fountain of Thy Word': Andrew Fuller as an Apologist*, Studies in Baptist History and Thought, vol. 6 (Carlisle, Cumbria, UK/Waynesboro, GA: Paternoster Press, 2004).

A note on the text and acknowledgements

Capitalization, biblical references, italicization, and some punctuation have been modernized in these texts of Fuller. I have also added paragraph divisions in Fuller's letter to George Charles Smith.

I am extremely thankful to Chance Faulkner for his vision in conceiving this work and seeing it through the press with Corey Hughes. I am also thankful for those who read Fuller with me in the Summer 2020 webinar: Nick Abraham, David Bissett, C.T. Eldridge, Chance Faulkner, Lisa Fang, Jacob Mathieu, Stephen McKay, Jordan Senécal, Matthew Sennholz, and Baiyu Andrew Song. Help on a few other items was provided by Dr. Chris Chun, D. Forrest Mills, Chris Fenner, and John Banks, Jr., for which I am extremely grateful. And I am indebted to Jared Skinner for drawing

---

[7] A second edition is forthcoming 2021 by H&E Publishing.

Introduction

my attention to Fuller's fabulous letter to Charles George Smith and to Candace Choy for typing it as well as for typing "To the Christian Females of Great Britain." Finally, I need to thank John Friesen, the CEO of Muskoka Bible Centre, for the privilege of four days and five nights on the lovely property of the Centre, where I was able to finish this book, surrounded by the gorgeous expanse of Muskoka.

Muskoka Bible Centre, Ontario
August 15, 2020

The pulpit of Kettering Baptist Church
from which Andrew Fuller preached

1
Confession of Faith[1]
(1783)

Introduction
When Andrew Fuller moved to Kettering to assume the pastoral leadership of the Particular Baptist work there, he delivered this confession on the occasion of his installation as this church's pastor on October 7, 1783. It is an interesting fact that, in the long eighteenth century, Particular Baptist ministers drew up their own individual confessions of faith rather than indicate their agreement to the *Second London Confession* (1677/1688), which had been ratified as the denominational statement of faith in 1689. Of course, these individual confessions were within the bounds of the theology of the *Second London Confession*, but this is a feature of Particular Baptist life that distinguishes them from other Reformed confessional traditions.

Confession of Faith
I. When I consider the heavens and the earth with their vast variety, it gives me reason to believe the existence of a God of infinite wisdom, power, and goodness that made and upholds them all. Had there been no written revelation of God given to us, I should have been without excuse, if I had denied a God or refused to glorify him as God.

II. Yet, considering the present state of mankind, I believe we needed a revelation of the mind of God to inform us more fully of his and our own character, of his designs towards us, and will

---

[1] From *The Last Remains of the Rev. Andrew Fuller: Sermons, Essays, Letters, and Other Miscellaneous Papers, not included in his Published Works*, ed. Joseph Belcher (Philadelphia, PA: American Baptist Publication Society, 1856), 209–217.

concerning us. And such a revelation I believe the Scriptures of the Old and New Testament to be, without excepting any one of its books, and a perfect rule of faith and practice. When I acknowledge it as a perfect rule of faith and practice, I mean to disclaim all other rules as binding on my conscience, and as well to acknowledge that if I err, either in faith or practice, from the rule, it will be my crime. For I have ever considered all deviations from divine rules to be criminal.

III. From this divine volume, I learn many things concerning God, which I could not have learned from the works of nature, and the same things in a more convincing light. Here I learn especially the infinitely amiable moral character of God. His holiness, justice, faithfulness, and goodness are here exhibited in such a light by his holy law and glorious gospel as is nowhere else to be seen.

Here, also, I learn that though God is one, yet he also is three—the Father, the Son, and the Holy Spirit. The idea which I think the Scriptures give us of each of the sacred three is that of person.

I believe the Son of God to be truly and properly God, equal with the Father and the Holy Spirit.

Everything I see in this sacred mystery appears to me above reason, but nothing contrary to it.

IV. I believe, from the same authority, that God created man in the image of his own glorious moral character, a proper subject of his moral government, with dispositions exactly suited to the law he was under and capacity equal to obey it to the uttermost against all temptations to the contrary. I believe if Adam, or any holy being, had had the making of a law for himself, he would have made just such an one as God's law is, for it would be the greatest of hardships to a holy being not to be allowed to love God with all his heart, and with all his soul, and all his mind.

V. I believe the conduct of man, in breaking the law of God, was most unreasonable and wicked in itself, as well as fatal in its consequences to the transgressor, and that sin is of such a nature that it deserves all the wrath and misery with which it is threatened, in this world, and in that which is to come.

VI. I believe the first sin of Adam was not merely personal, but that he stood as our representative. So that when he fell, we fell in him, and became liable to condemnation and death. And what is more, [we] are all born into the world with a vile propensity to sin against God.

I own there are some things in these subjects, which appear to me profound and awful. But seeing God hath so plainly revealed them in his Word, especially in the fifth chapter of the epistle to the Romans, I dare not but bow my shallow conceptions to the unerring testimony of God, not doubting but that he will clear his own character sufficiently at the last day. At the same time, I know of no other system that represents these subjects in a more rational light.

VII. I believe, as I before stated, that men are now born and grow up with a vile propensity to moral evil, and that herein lies their inability to keep God's law, and as such, it is a moral and a criminal inability. Were they but of a right disposition of mind, there is nothing now in the law of God but what they could perform; but, being wholly under the dominion of sin, they have no heart remaining for God, but are full of wicked aversion to him. Their very mind and conscience are defiled. Their ideas of the excellence of good and of the evil of sin are as it were obliterated.

These are subjects which seem to me of very great importance. I conceive that the whole Arminian, Socinian, and Antinomian systems, so far as I understand them, rest upon the supposition of these principles being false. So that, if it should be found, at last, that God is an infinitely excellent being, worthy of being loved with all the love which his law requires; that, as such, his law is entirely fair and equitable and that for God to have required less, would have been denying himself to be what he is; and if it should appear, at last, that man is utterly lost, and lies absolutely at the discretion of God; then, I think it is easy to prove, the whole of these systems must fall to the ground. If men, on account of sin, lie at the discretion of God, the equity, and even necessity, of predestination cannot be denied, and so the Arminian system falls. If the law of God is right and good, and arises from the very nature of God, Antinomianism cannot stand. And if we are such great sinners, we need a great Saviour, infinitely greater than the Socinian Saviour.

VIII. From what I have said, it must be supposed that I believe the doctrine of eternal personal election and predestination. However, I believe that though in the choice of the elect, God had no motive out of himself, yet it was not so in respect to punishing the rest. What has been usually, but perhaps, improperly, called the decree of reprobation, I consider as nothing more than the divine determination to punish sin, in certain cases, in the person of the sinner.

IX. I believe that the fall of man did not at all disconcert the great Eternal, but that he had from eternity formed a plan upon the supposition of that event (as well knowing that so it would be) and that, in this everlasting covenant, as it is called, the Sacred Three (speaking after the manner of men) stipulated with each other for the bringing about their vast and glorious design.

X. The unfolding of this glorious plan to view, I believe, has been a gradual work from the beginning. First, it was hinted to our first parents, in the promise of the woman's seed. Then, by the institution of sacrifices, by types, prophecies, and promises, it was carried on throughout the Mosaic dispensation. At length the Son of God appeared, took our nature, obeyed the law, and endured the curse, and hereby made full and proper atonement for the sins of his own elect, rose again from the dead, commissioned his apostles to go into all the world and preach his gospel, and then triumphantly ascended above all heavens, where he sitteth at the right hand of God, interceding for his people, and governing the world in subserviency to their welfare, till he shall come a second time to judge the world.

I cannot reflect upon this glorious procedure, with its all-glorious Author, without emotions of wonder and gratitude. As a workman, he might be truly said to have "his work before him!" At once he glorified the injured character of God and confounded the devil—destroyed sin and saved the sinner.

XI. I believe that such is the excellence of this way of salvation that everyone who hears, or has opportunity to hear it proclaimed in the gospel, is bound to repent of his sin, believe, approve, and embrace it with all his heart; to consider himself, as he really is, a vile, lost sinner; to reject all pretensions to life in any other way; and to cast himself upon Christ that he may be saved in this way of God's devising. This I think to be true faith, which whoever have, I believe, will certainly be saved.

XII. But, though the way of salvation is in itself so glorious, that a man must be an enemy to God, to mankind, and to himself, not to approve it, yet I believe the pride, ignorance, enmity, and love to sin in men, is such that they will not come to Christ for life; but, in spite of all the calls and threatenings of God, will go on, till they sink into eternal perdition. Hence, I believe, arises the necessity of an almighty work of God the Spirit, to new-model the whole soul, to form in us new principles or dispositions, or, as the Scriptures call it, to give us "a new heart and a right spirit."[2] I think, had we not first degenerated, we had stood in no need of being regenerated. But as we are by nature depraved, we must be born again. The influence of the Spirit of God, in this work, I believe to be always effectual.

XIII. I believe the change that takes place in a person at the time of his believing in the Lord Jesus Christ, is not only real, but relative. Before our believing in Christ, we are considered and treated by God, as a lawgiver, as under condemnation; but having fled to him

---

[2] Ezekiel 18:31. Cf. also Ezekiel 36:26.

for refuge, the law, as to its condemning power, hath no more dominion over us, but we are treated, even by God the judge, as in a state of justification. The subject-matter of justification, I believe to be nothing of our own moral excellence, but the righteousness of Christ alone, imputed to us and received by faith.

Also, I believe that before we believe in Christ, notwithstanding the secret purpose of God in our favour, we are considered by the moral governor of the world as aliens, as children of wrath, even as others; but that, on our believing on his Son, we are considered as no more strangers and foreigners, but are admitted into his family and have power, or privilege, to become the sons of God.

XIV. I believe that those who are effectually called of God never fall away so as to perish everlastingly, but persevere in holiness till they arrive at endless happiness.

XV. I believe it is the duty of every minister of Christ plainly and faithfully to preach the gospel to all who will hear it. And, as I believe the inability of men to spiritual things to be wholly of the moral, and therefore of the criminal kind—and that it is their duty to love the Lord Jesus Christ and trust in him for salvation, though they do not—I, therefore, believe free and solemn addresses, invitations, calls, and warnings to them, to be not only consistent, but directly adapted, as means in the hands of the Spirit of God to bring them to Christ. I consider it as a part of my duty, which I could not omit without being guilty of the blood of souls.

XVI. I believe the ordinances which Christ, as king of Zion, has instituted for his church to be found in, throughout the gospel day, are especially two, namely, Baptism and the Lord's Supper. I believe the subjects of both to be those who profess repentance towards God and faith towards our Lord Jesus Christ, and on such I consider them as incumbent duties. I believe that it is essential to Christian baptism that it be by immersion, or burying the person in water, in the name of the Father, the Son, and the Holy Ghost. I likewise believe baptism as administered by the primitive church to be prerequisite to church communion. Hence, I judge what is called strict communion to be consistent with the Word of God.

XVII. Although I disclaim personal holiness as having any share in our justification, I consider it absolutely necessary to salvation, for without it "no man shall see the Lord."

XVIII. I believe the soul of man is created immortal, and that, when the body dies, the soul returns to God who gave it and there receives an immediate sentence, either to a state of happiness or misery, there to remain till the resurrection of the dead.

XIX. As I said that the development of God's plan has been gradual from the beginning, so I believe this graduation will be beautifully and gloriously carried on. I firmly and joyfully believe that the kingdom of Christ will yet be gloriously extended by the pouring out of God's Spirit upon the ministry of the Word. And I consider this as an event, for the arrival of which it becomes all God's servants and churches most ardently to pray! It is one of the chief springs of my joy in this "day of small things" that it will not be so always.

XX. Finally, I believe that Christ will come a second time, not as before, to save the world, but to judge the world. There, in the presence of an assembled universe, every son and daughter of Adam shall appear at God's tremendous bar and give an account of the things done in the body. There sinners, especially those who have rejected Christ, God's way of salvation, will be convicted, confounded, and righteously condemned! These shall go away into everlasting punishment. But the righteous, who through grace have embraced Christ and followed him whithersoever he went, shall follow him there likewise and enter with him into the eternal joy of their Lord. This solemn event, I own, on some accounts strikes me with trembling. Yet, on others, I cannot but look on it with a mixture of joy. When I consider it as the period when God will be vindicated from all the hard thoughts which ungodly sinners have indulged and the hard speeches which they have spoken against him; when all wrongs shall be made right, truth brought to light, and justice done where none here could be obtained; when the whole empire of sin, misery, and death shall sink like a mill-stone into the sea of eternal oblivion and never rise more. When, I say, I consider it in this view, I cannot but look upon it as an object of joy and wish my time may be spent in this world in "looking for and hasting unto the coming of the day of God."[3]

---

[3] 2 Peter 3:12.

Questions

1. Why are the Scriptures necessary? How does Fuller view the Bible?
2. What do the Scriptures teach about God?
3. What does it mean to be a human being?
4. What does Fuller mean by saying that man's inability to obey God is "a moral and a criminal inability"?
5. Why does Fuller believe that "the whole Arminian, Socinian, and Antinomian systems" are not adequate explanations of the doctrine of salvation?
6. How does Fuller understand the doctrine of reprobation?
7. What does saving faith entail?
8. What is the "almighty work of God the Spirit" that Fuller considers necessary? Why is it an absolute necessity?
9. What is "the duty of every minister of Christ"?
10. How many ordinances are there? What is baptism? What is its relationship to the Lord's Supper? Does Fuller delineate the nature of the Lord's Supper?
11. What gives Fuller joy?

John Owen

2
An Enquiry into the Causes of Declension in Religion, with the Means of Revival[1] (1785)

Introduction

One the earliest usages of the term "revival" for the renewal of a Christian community comes in a letter of the Puritan theologian John Owen (1616-1683), who deeply influenced Andrew Fuller's early thought. Writing in a 1674 letter to Charles Fleetwood (c.1618-1692), Owen urged him "to labour after spiritual revivals."[2] In this circular letter that Fuller drew up in 1785 for the Northamptonshire Association of Baptist churches—such letters were sent to all of the churches in the Association after their annual meeting that was normally held in the week of Pentecost—Fuller delineated why Christian churches and communities decline and how they can experience genuine revival.

An Enquiry into the Causes of Declension in Religion

Grace be to you, and peace from God our Father, and from the Lord Jesus Christ.

Dearly beloved brethren,

Through the good hand of our God upon us we met together according to appointment and enjoyed the pleasure of an agreeable

---

[1] From *The Complete Works of the Rev. Andrew Fuller*, ed. Joseph Belcher (1845, Harrisonburg, VA: Sprinkle Publications, 1988), *Works*, III, 318-324.

[2] John Owen, Letter to Charles Fleetwood, July 8, [1674], in *The Correspondence of John Owen*, ed. Peter Toon (Cambridge: James Clarke, 1970), 159.

interview with several of our dear friends and brethren in the Lord. We trust also that our God was with us in the different stages of the opportunity. The letters from the several churches, which were attended to the first evening of our meeting together, afforded us matter for pain and pleasure. Two of the associate churches continue destitute of the stated means of grace, others are tried with things of an uncomfortable nature, and most complain of the want of a spirit of fervour and constancy in the ways of God. Yet, on the other hand, we met with some things which afforded us pleasure. Many of our congregations are well attended; a spirit of desire after the Word is, we think, upon the increase; nor are our labours, we hope, altogether in vain, as the work of the Lord, in a way of conversion, appears to be carrying on, though not in instances very remarkable.

'Tis true we have reason to bewail our own and others' declensions, yet we are not, upon the whole, discouraged. It affords us no little satisfaction to hear in what manner the monthly prayer meetings which were proposed in our letter of last year have been carried on, and how God has been evidently present in those meetings, stirring up the hearts of his people to wrestle hard with him for the revival of his blessed cause. Though as to the number of members there is no increase this year, but something of the contrary; yet a spirit of prayer in some measure being poured out more than balances in our account for this defect. We cannot but hope, wherever we see a spirit of earnest prayer generally and perseveringly prevail, that God has some good in reserve, which in his own time he will graciously bestow.

But while we rejoice to see such a spirit of united prayer, we must not stop here, brethren, lest in so doing we stop short. If we would hope for the blessing of God upon us, there must be added to this a spirit of earnest enquiry into the causes of our declensions, and a hearty desire and endeavour for their removal. When Israel could not go forward, but were smitten by the men of Ai, Joshua and the elders of the people prostrated themselves before the Lord. In this they did well; but this was not sufficient "Get thee up," said the Lord to his servant—"wherefore liest thou thus upon thy face? Israel hath sinned—Up, sanctify the people—and search for the accursed thing!"[3] This, it is apprehended, is the case with us, as well as it was with Israel; and this must be our employment as well as theirs. With a view to assist you, brethren, and ourselves with you, in this very necessary enquiry, we appropriate the present letter to pointing out of some of those evils which we apprehend to be causes of that declension of which so many complain, and the means of their removal.

The first thing that we shall request you to make inquiry about is, whether there is not a great degree of contentedness with a mere superficial acquaintance with the gospel, without entering into its spirit and end; and whether this be not one great cause of the declension complained of. In the apostles' time, and in all times, grace and peace have ever been multiplied by the knowledge of God; and, in proportion as this has been neglected, those have always declined. If we are sanctified by the Word of truth, then, as this Word is received or disrelished, the work of sanctification must be supposed to rise or fall. We may give a sort of idle assent to the truths of God, which amounts to little more than taking it for granted that they are true, and thinking no more about them, unless somebody opposes us; but this will not influence the heart and life, and yet it seems to be nearly the whole of what many attain to, or seek after.

We maintain the doctrine of one infinitely glorious God; but do we realize the amiableness of his character? If we did, we could not avoid loving him with our heart, and soul, and mind, and strength. We hold the doctrine of the universal depravity of mankind; but do we enter into its evil nature and awful tendency? If we did the one, how much lower should we lie before God, and how much more

---

[3] Joshua 7:10–13, passim.

should we be filled with a self-loathing spirit? If the other, how should we feel for our fellow sinners? How earnest should we be to use all means, and have all means used, if it might please God thereby to pluck them as brands out of the burning?

We hold the doctrine of a Trinity of persons in the Godhead; but do we cordially enter into the glorious economy of redemption, wherein the conduct of the sacred Three is most gloriously displayed? Surely if we did, the grace of our Lord Jesus Christ, the love of God, and the communion of the Holy Ghost would be with us more than it is.

We avow the doctrines of free, sovereign, and efficacious grace; but do we generally feel the grace therein discovered? If we did, how low should we lie? How grateful should we be? We should seldom think of their sovereign and discriminating nature, without considering how justly God might have left us all to have had our own will, and followed our own ways; to have continued to increase our malady, and despise the only remedy. Did we properly enter into these subjects, we could not think of a great Saviour, and a great salvation, without loathing ourselves for being such great sinners; nor of what God had done for and given to us, without longing to give him our little all, and feeling an habitual desire to do something for him. If we realized our redemption by the blood of Christ, it would be natural for us to consider ourselves as bought with a price, and therefore not our own, "a price, all price beyond!" O, could we enter into this, we should readily discern the force and propriety of our body and spirit being his; his indeed, dearly bought, and justly due!

Finally, we all profess to believe the vanity of this life and its enjoyments, and the infinitely superior value of that above; but do we indeed enter into these things? If we did, surely we should have more of heavenly-mindedness, and less of criminal attachment to the world.

Causes of Declension

It is owing in a great degree to this contentment with a superficial knowledge of things, without entering into the spirit of them, that we so often hear the truths of the gospel spoken of with a tone of disgust, calling them "dry doctrines"! Whereas gospel truths, if preached in their native simplicity, and received with understanding and cordiality, are the grand source of all well-grounded consolation. We know of no consolation worth receiving but what arises from the influence of truth upon the mind. Christ's words are spirit and life to them who hunger and thirst after them, or have a heart to live upon them; and could we but more thoroughly enter into this way of living, we should find the doctrines of the gospel, instead of being dry, to be what they were in the days of Moses, who declared, "My doctrine shall drop as the rain, my speech shall distil as the dew; as the small rain upon the tender herb, and as the showers upon the grass."[4] O brethren, may it be our and your concern not to float upon the surface of Christianity, but to enter into the spirit of it! "For this cause" an apostle bowed his knees "to the Father of our Lord Jesus Christ," that we might "comprehend the breadth, and length, and depth, and height"[5] of things; and for this cause we also wish to bow our knees, knowing that it is by this, if at all, that we are "filled with all the fulness of God."[6]

Another thing which we apprehend to be a great cause of declension is, a contentedness with present attainments, without aspiring after eminence in grace and holiness. If we may judge of people's thoughts and aims by the general tenor of their conduct, there seems to be much of a contentment with about so much religion as is thought necessary to constitute them good men, and that will just suffice to carry them to heaven; without aiming by a course of more than ordinary services to glorify God in their day and generation. We

---

[4] Deuteronomy 32:2.
[5] Ephesians 3:8.
[6] Ephesians 3:14–19.

profess to do what we do with a view to glorify God, and not to be saved by it; but is it so indeed? Do these things look like it? How is it, too, that the positive institutions of Christ are treated with so little regard? Whence is it that we hear such language as this so often as we do: "Such a duty, and such an ordinance, is not essential to salvation—we may never be baptized in water, or become church members, and yet go to heaven as well as they that are?"

It is to be feared the old puritanical way of devoting ourselves wholly to be the Lord's, resigning up our bodies, souls, gifts, time, property, with all we have and are to serve him, and frequently renewing these covenants before him, is now awfully neglected. This was to make a business of religion, a life's work, and not merely an accidental affair, occurring but now and then, and what must be attended to only when we can spare time from other engagements. Few seem to aim, pray, and strive after eminent love to God and one another. Many appear to be contented if they can but remember the time when they had such love in exercise, and then, tacking to it the notion of perseverance without the thing, they go on and on, satisfied, it seems, if they do but make shift just to get to heaven at last, without much caring how. If we were in a proper spirit, the question with us would not so much be, "What must I do for God?" as, "What can I do for God?" A servant that heartily loves his master counts it a privilege to be employed by him, yea, an honour to be intrusted with any of his concerns.

If it is inquired, "What then is to be done? wherein in particular can we glorify God more than we have done?" We answer by asking: Is there no room for amendment? Have we been sufficiently earnest and constant in private prayer? Are there none of us that have opportunities to set apart particular times to pray for the effusion of the Holy Spirit? Can we do no more than we have done in instructing our families? Are there none of our dependants, workmen, or neighbours that we might speak to, at least so far as to ask them to go and

CAUSES OF DECLENSION

hear the gospel? Can we rectify nothing in our tempers and behaviour in the world, so as better to recommend religion? Cannot we watch more? Cannot we save a little more of our substance to give to the poor? In a word, is there no room or possibility left for our being more meek, loving, and resembling the blessed Jesus than we have been?

To glorify God, and recommend by our example the religion of the meek and lowly Jesus, are the chief ends for which it is worth while to live; but do we sufficiently pursue these ends? Even these chief ends of our existence, are they in any good degree so much as kept in view? Ah, what have we done for God in the towns, villages, and families where we reside? Christians are said to be the light of the world, and the salt of the earth: do we answer these characters? Is the world enlightened by us? Does a savour of Christ accompany our spirit and conversation? Our business, as Christians, is practically to be holding forth the Word of life. Have we, by our earnestness, sufficiently held forth its importance, or by our chaste conversation, coupled with fear, its holy tendency? Have we all along, by a becoming firmness of spirit, made it evident that religion is no low, mean, or dastardly business? Have we by a cheerful complacency in God's service, gospel, and providence sufficiently held forth the excellency of his government and the happy tendency of his holy religion? Doubtless, the most holy and upright Christians in these matters will find great cause for reflection, and room for amendment; but are there not many who scarcely ever think about them, or, if they do, it only amounts to this, to sigh, and go backward, resting satisfied with a few lifeless complaints, without any real and abiding efforts to have things otherwise?

Another cause of declension, we apprehend, is making the religion of others our standard, instead of the Word of God. The Word of God is the only safe rule we have to go by, either in judging what is real religion, or what exertions and services for God are incumbent upon us. As it is unsafe to conclude ourselves real Christians because we may have such feelings as we have heard spoken of by some whom we account good men, so it is unjust to conclude that we have religion enough because we may suppose ourselves to be equal to the generality of those that now bear that character. What if they be good men? They are not our standard and what if their conversation in general be such as gives them a reputation in the religious world? Christ did not say, "Learn of them," but, "Learn of me."[7] Or if in a measure we are allowed to follow them who through faith and patience inherit the promises, still it is with this restriction, as far as they are followers of Christ.

Alas, how much is the professing part of mankind governed by ill example! If the question turns upon religious diligence, as: How often shall I attend at the house of God—once or twice on the Lord's day? Or how frequently shall I give my company at church meetings, opportunities for prayer, and such like? Is not the answer commonly governed by what others do in these cases, rather than by what is right in itself? So, if it turns on liberality, the question is not, "What am I able to spare in this case, consistent with all other obligations?" but, "What does Mr. such a one give? I shall do the same as he does." Something of this kind may not be wrong, as a degree of proportion among friends is desirable; but if carried to too great lengths, we must beware lest our attention to precedent should so far exclude principle in the affair as to render even what we do unacceptable in the sight of God. So, if the question turns on any particular piece of conduct, whether it be defensible or not, instead of searching the Bible, and praying to be led in the narrow way of truth and righteousness, how common is it to hear such language as this: "Such and such good men do so; surely, therefore, there can be no great harm in it!" In short, great numbers appear to be quite satisfied if they are

---

[7] Matthew 11:29.

but about as strict and as holy as other people with whom they are connected.

Many ill effects appear evidently to arise from this quarter. Hence it is that, for the want of bringing our religion and religious life to the test of God's holy Word, we are in general so wretchedly deficient in a sense of our vast and constant defects, have no spirit to press forward, but go on and on, without repentance for them, or so much as a thought of doing otherwise. Hence also there is so much vanity and spiritual pride among us. While we content ourselves with barely keeping pace with one another, we may all become wretched idlers, and loose walkers; and yet, as one is about as good as another, each may think highly of himself; whereas, bring him and his companions with him to the glass of God's holy Word, and if they have any sensibility left, they must see their odious picture, abhor themselves, and feel their former conduct as but too much resembling that of a company of evil conspirators who kept each other in countenance. Finally, to this it may be ascribed in part that so many are constantly waxing worse and worse, more and more loose and careless in their spirit and conduct. For those who are contented not to do better than other people, generally allow themselves to do a little worse. An imitator is scarcely ever known to equal an original in the good, but generally exceeds him in the bad; not only in imitating his feelings, but adding others to their number. If we would resemble any great and good man, we must do as he does, and that is, keep our eye upon the mark, and follow Christ as our model. It is by this means that he has attained to be what he is. Here we shall be in no danger of learning anything amiss; and truly we have failings now of our own, in not conforming to the model, without deriving any more from the imperfections of the model itself.

Once more, the want of considering the consequences of our own good and evil conduct is, we apprehend, another great cause of declension in many people. It is common for people on many occasions to think within themselves in some such manner as this: "What signify my faults, or my efforts? They can weigh but little for or against the public good. What will my prayers avail? And what great loss will be sustained by an individual occasionally omitting the duty of prayer, or attendance on a church meeting, or it may be the public worship and ordinances of God? And what consequences will follow if one be a little now and then off one's watch, nobody is perfect?" etc. This, and a great deal more such horrid Atheism, it is to be feared, if a thorough search were made, would be found to lie at the bottom of our common departures from God.

If, when an army goes forth to engage the enemy, every soldier were to reason with himself thus: "Of what great consequence will my services be? It is but little execution that I can do; it will make but very little difference, therefore, if I desert or stand neuter—there are enow to fight without me"—what would be the consequence? Would such reasoning be admitted? Was it admitted in the case of the Reubenites, who cowardly abode by their sheep-folds while their brethren jeoparded their lives upon the high places in the field? Was not Meroz cursed with a bitter curse because its inhabitants came not forth to the help of the Lord in the day of the mighty?[8] If an army would hope to obtain the victory, every man should act as if the whole issue of the battle depended upon his conduct: so, if ever things go well in a religious view, it will be when every one is concerned to act as if he were the only one that remained on God's side.

We may think the efforts of an individual to be trifling; but, dear brethren, let not this atheistical spirit prevail over us. It is the same spawn with that cast forth in the days of Job, when they asked concerning the Almighty, "What profit shall we have if we pray unto him?" At this rate Abraham might have forborne interceding for Sodom, and Daniel for his brethren of the captivity. James also must be mistaken in saying that the prayer of a single, individual righteous

---

[8] Judges 5:15–16, 23.

man availeth much. Ah, brethren, this spirit is not from above, but cometh of an evil heart of unbelief departing from the living God! Have done with that bastard humility, that teaches you such a sort of thinking low of your own prayers and exertions for God as to make you decline them, or at least to be slack or indifferent in them! Great things frequently rise from small beginnings. Some of the greatest good that has ever been done in the world has been set a going by the efforts of an individual. Witness the Christianizing of a great part of the heathen world by the labours of a Paul, and the glorious Reformation from popery began by the struggles of a Luther.

It is impossible to tell what good may result from one earnest wrestling with God, from one hearty exertion in his cause, or from one instance of a meek and lowly spirit, overcoming evil with good. Though there is nothing in our doings from which we could look for such great things, yet God is pleased frequently to crown our poor services with infinite reward. Such conduct may be, and often has been, the means of the conversion and eternal salvation of souls; and who that has any Christianity in him would not reckon this reward enough? A realizing sense of these things would stir us all up; ministers to preach the gospel to every creature, private Christians, situated in this or that dark town or village, to use all means to have it preached, and both to recommend it to all around by a meek and unblemished conversation.

Again, we may think the faults of an individual to be trifling, but they are not so. For the crime of Achan the army of Israel suffered a defeat, and the whole camp could not go forward. Let us tremble at the thought of being a dead weight to the society of which we are members! Besides, the awful tendency of such conduct is seen in its contagious influence. If people continue to be governed by example, as they certainly will in a great degree, then there is no knowing what the consequences will be, nor where they will end. A single defect or slip, of which we may think but little at the time, may be copied by our children, servants, neighbours, or friends, over and over again; yea, it may be transmitted to posterity, and pleaded as a precedent for evil when we are no more! Thus it may kindle a fire which, if we ourselves are saved from it, may nevertheless burn to the lowest hell, and aggravate the everlasting misery of many around us, who are "flesh of our flesh, and bone of our bone!"[9]

These, brethren, we apprehend, are some of the causes, among many others, which have produced these declensions which you and we lament. But what do we say? Do we indeed lament them? If we do, it will be natural for us to inquire, "What shall we do? What means can be used towards their removal, and a happy revival?" If this be now indeed the object of our inquiry, we cannot do better than to attend to the advice of the great Head of the church to a backsliding people: "Remember from whence thou art fallen, and repent, and do thy first works. ... Be watchful, and strengthen the things that remain that are ready to die. ... Remember how thou hast received and heard, and hold fast, and repent!"[10] Particularly:

First, let us recollect the best periods of the Christian church, and compare them with the present; and the best parts of our own life, if we know when they were, and compare then with what we now are. A recollection of the disinterested zeal and godly simplicity of the primitive Christians, and their successors in after-ages, millions of whom, in Christ's cause, loved not their lives unto death, would surely make us loathe ourselves for our detestable lukewarmness. As Protestants, let us think of the fervent zeal and holy piety of our Reformers; think what objects they grasped, what difficulties they encountered, and what ends they obtained. As Protestant Dissenters, let us reflect on the spirit and conduct of our puritan and nonconforming ancestors. Think how they served God at the expense of all that was clear to them in this world, and laid the foundation of our

---

[9] Genesis 2:23.
[10] Revelation 2:5; 3:2–3.

churches in woods, and dens, and caves of the earth. Say, too, was their love to God more than need be? Is the importance of things abated since their death? Might not they have pleaded the danger and cruelty of the times in excuse for a non-appearance for God, with much more seeming plausibility than we can excuse our spirit of hateful indifference? O let us remember whence we are fallen, and repent!

As to our own lives, if we are real Christians, probably we can remember times wherein the great concerns of salvation seemed to eclipse all other objects. We covenanted with God—we resigned over all to him—we loved to be his, wholly his, rather than our own—we were willing to do any thing, or become any thing, that should glorify his name. And is it so now? No! But why not? What iniquity have we found in him, that we are gone away backward? "O my people, saith the Lord, what have I done unto thee? wherein have I wearied thee? Testify against me!"[11] Have I been a hard master, or a churlish father, or a faithless friend? Have I not been patient enough with you, or generous enough towards you? Could I have done any thing more for you that I have not done? Was the covenant you made with me a hard bargain? Was it hard on your side for me to be made sin, who knew no sin, that you might be made the righteousness of God in me? Were the rewards of my service such as you could not live upon? Is it better with you now than then? O Christian reader, pause awhile, lay aside the paper, and retire before God. Reflect, and pour out thy soul before him. Say unto him, "O Lord, righteousness belongeth unto thee, but unto us confusion of face."[12] Thus, thus, remember whence thou art fallen, and repent!

But do not stop here: think it not sufficient that we lament and mourn over our departures from God; we must return to him with full purpose of heart. "Strengthen the things that remain which are

---

[11] Micah 6:3.
[12] Daniel 9:7.

ready to die."[13] Cherish a greater love to the truths of God—pay an invariable regard to the discipline of his house—cultivate love to one another—frequently mingle souls by frequently assembling yourselves together—encourage a meek, humble, and savoury spirit, rather than a curious one. These are some of the things among us that are "ready to die." To this it is added, "Do thy first works."[14] Fill up your places in God's worship with that earnestness and constancy as when you were first seeking after the salvation of your souls—flee from those things which conscience, in its most tender and best informed state, durst not meddle with, though since perhaps they may have become trifling in your eyes—walk in your family, in the world, and in the church, with God always before you—live in love, meekness, and forbearance with one another—whatever your hands find you to do, "do it with all your might,"[15] seeking to promote, by all means, the present and eternal welfare of all around you.

Finally, brethren, let us not forget to intermingle prayer with all we do. Our need of God's Holy Spirit to enable us to do any thing, and every thing, truly good, should excite us to this. Without his blessing all means are without efficacy, and every effort for revival will be in vain. Constantly and earnestly, therefore, let us approach his throne. Take all occasions especially for closet prayer; here, if any where, we shall get fresh strength, and maintain a life of communion with God. Our Lord Jesus used frequently to retire into a mountain alone for prayer. He, therefore, that is a follower of Christ, must follow him in this important duty.

Dearly beloved brethren, farewell! "Unto him that is able to keep you from falling, and to present you faultless before the presence of his glory with exceeding joy, to the only wise God our Saviour, be

---

[13] Revelation 3:2.
[14] Revelation 2:5.
[15] Ecclesiastes 5:9; Colossians 3:23.

glory and majesty, dominion and power, both now and ever. Amen."[16]

---

[16] Jude 24–25.

Questions

1. In one sentence define "religion" and "revival." Would you describe these two words as positive terms or negative ones? Are they positive or negative for Fuller?
2. What has been transpiring in the churches of this Baptist Association?
3. What is the "spirit of prayer in some measure being poured out"? Why is Fuller sanguine about the impact of this on the churches of his Association?
4. What is the immediate purpose of this circular letter?
5. What does Fuller identify as the first matter that needs to be addressed in seeking revival? Enumerate the various illustrations that Fuller gives to substantiate his point here. For example, he mentions the Association's commitment to "the doctrine of a Trinity of persons in the Godhead." What is the practical import of holding to this truth?
6. Why does Fuller not regard these central truths of the Christian Faith as "dry doctrines"?
7. Briefly explain how this sentence sums up the core of Fuller's argument in these first couple of pages: "We know of no consolation worth receiving but what arises from the influence of truth upon the mind."
8. What is the second matter that Fuller sees as essential?
9. What is "old puritanical way" that Fuller believes is necessary for his day?
10. Outline the difference between these two questions: "What must I do for God?" and "What can I do for God?"
11. What are the specific things Fuller believes need to be done in answer to the question, "What can I do for God?"
12. What text might Fuller be drawing this statement from: "To glorify God, and recommend by our example the religion of the meek

Qualifications & Encouragement

and lowly Jesus, are the chief ends for which it is worth while to live"?

13. What is a third area of declension? How does Fuller view the Scriptures?
14. How does Fuller answer the feeling that "the efforts of an individual ...[are] trifling"? Why is this significant as a cause of declension?
15. How can remembering the past be helpful in seeking revival?
16. What does Fuller understand by returning to God with "full purpose of heart"?
17. Why is prayer vital?

Barnabas
(from William Cave, *Apostolici: or, The History of the Lives, Acts, Death, and Martyrdoms of those Who were Contemporary with, or immediately Succeeded the Apostles*, 4th ed. [London, 1716])

3
The Qualifications and Encouragement of a Faithful Minister, illustrated by the Character and Success of Barnabas[1] (1787)

Introduction

Eighteenth-century ordinations of Particular Baptist ministers usually included two sermons, one to the man being ordained and one to his congregation. Fuller was in regular demand to preach on such occasions, and as such has left us the largest corpus of Baptist ordination sermons of his era. As one nineteenth-century editor put it, Fuller "took much pleasure in assisting young ministers in their theological inquiries, for which he was eminently qualified, and also in encouraging useful gifts."[2] This sermon was preached at the installation of Robert Fawkner as the pastor of Thorn Baptist Church, Bedfordshire, on October 31, 1787.

---

[1] From Michael A.G. Haykin and Brian Croft with Ian H. Clary, *Being a Pastor: A Conversation with Andrew Fuller* (Darlington, Co. Durham: EP Books, 2019), 87–107. This volume contains nineteen ordination sermons.

[2] Anonymous, "Preface" to *The Preacher: or Sketches of Original Sermons, chiefly selected from the Manuscripts of Two Eminent Divines of the Last Century, for the Use of Lay Preachers and Young Ministers* (Philadelphia, PA: J. Whetham, 1838), v.

35

The Qualifications and Encouragement of a Faithful Minister

> "He was a good man, and full of the Holy Spirit, and of faith; and much people was added to the Lord"[3]

My dear brother,

It is a very important work to which you are this day set apart. I feel the difficulty of your situation. You need both counsel and encouragement; I wish I were better able to administer both. In what I may offer, I am persuaded you will allow me to be free; and understand me, not as assuming any authority or superiority over you, but only as saying that to you which I wish to consider as equally addressed to myself.

Out of a variety of topics that might afford a lesson for a Christian minister, my thoughts have turned, on this occasion, upon that of example. Example has a great influence upon the human mind: examples from Scripture especially, wherein characters the most illustrious in their day, for gifts, grace, and usefulness, are drawn with the pencil of inspiration, have an assimilating tendency. Viewing these, under a divine blessing, we form some just conceptions of the nature and importance of our work, are led to reflect upon our own defects, and feel the fire of holy emulation kindling in our bosoms.

The particular example, my brother, which I wish to recommend to your attention is that of Barnabas, that excellent servant of Christ and companion of the apostle Paul. You will find his character particularly given in the words I have just read.

Were we to examine the life of this great and good man, as related in other parts of Scripture, we should find the character here given him abundantly confirmed. He seems to have been one of that great company who, through the preaching of Peter and the other apostles, submitted to Christ soon after his ascension; and he gave

---

[3] Acts 11:24.

Qualifications & Encouragement

early proof of his love to him, by selling his possessions, and laying the price at the feet of the apostles for the support of his infant cause. As he loved Christ, so he loved his people. He appears to have possessed much of the tender and affectionate, on account of which he was called "Barnabas—a son of consolation."[4] Assiduous in discovering and encouraging the first dawnings of God's work, he was the first person that introduced Saul into the company of the disciples. The next news that we hear of him is in the passage which I have selected. Tidings came to the ears of the church at Jerusalem of the Word of the Lord being prosperous at Antioch, in Syria. The church at Jerusalem was the mother church, and felt a concern for others, like that of a tender mother towards her infant offspring. The young converts at Antioch wanted a nursing father; and who so proper to be sent as Barnabas? He goes; and, far from envying the success of others, who had laboured before him, he "was glad to see the grace of God" so evidently appear; "and exhorted them all that with purpose of heart they would cleave unto the Lord."[5] As a preacher, he does not seem to have been equal to the apostle Paul; yet so far was he from caring about being eclipsed by Paul's superior abilities, that he went in search of him, and brought him to Antioch, to assist him in the work of the Lord. It may well be said of such a character, that he was a "good man, and full of the Holy Spirit, and of faith."[6] Oh that we had more such ministers in the church at this day! Oh that we ourselves were like him! Might we not hope, if that were the case, that, according to God's usual manner of working, more people would be added to the Lord?

There are three things, we see, which are said of Barnabas in a way of commendation: he was "a good man, full of the Holy Spirit, and of faith." Thus far he is held up for our example: a fourth is

---

[4] Acts 4:36.
[5] Acts 11:23.
[6] Acts 11:24.

added, concerning the effects which followed: "and much people was added unto the Lord."[7] This seems to be held up for our encouragement. Permit me, my dear brother, to request your candid attention, while I attempt to review these great qualities in Barnabas, and by every motive to enforce them upon you.

I. He was a good man. It were easy to prove the necessity of a person being a good man, in order to his properly engaging in the work of the ministry: Christ would not commit his sheep but to one that loved him. But on this remark I shall not enlarge. I have no reason to doubt, my brother, but that God has given you an understanding to know him that is true, and a heart to love him in sincerity; I trust, therefore, such an attempt, on this occasion, is needless. Nor does it appear to me to be the meaning of the evangelist. It is not barely meant of Barnabas that he was a regenerate man, though that is implied; but it denotes that he was eminently good. We use the word so in common conversation. If we would describe one that more than ordinarily shines in piety, meekness, and kindness, we know not how to speak of him better than to say, with a degree of emphasis: "He is a good man." After this eminence in goodness, brother, may it be your concern, and mine, daily to aspire!

Perhaps, indeed, we may have sometimes heard this epithet used with a sneer. Persons who take pleasure in treating others with contempt will frequently, with a kind of proud pity, speak in this manner: "Aye, such a one is a good man;" leaving it implied that goodness is but an indifferent qualification, unless it be accompanied with greatness. But these things ought not to be. The apostle Paul did not value himself upon those things wherein he differed from other Christians; but upon that which he possessed in common with them—charity, or Christian love:

---

[7] Acts 11:24.

QUALIFICATIONS & ENCOURAGEMENT

Though I speak with the tongues of men and of angels, and have not charity, I am become as sounding brass, or a tinkling cymbal. And though I have the gift of prophecy, and understand all mysteries, and all knowledge; and though I have all faith, so that I could remove mountains, and have not charity; I am nothing.[8]

My dear brother, value the character of a good man in all the parts of your employment; and, above all, in those things which the world counts great and estimable. More particularly,

1. Value it at home in your family. If you walk not closely with God there, you will be ill able to work for him elsewhere. You have lately become the head of a family. Whatever charge it shall please God, in the course of your life, to place under your care, I trust it will be your concern to recommend Christ and the gospel to them, walk circumspectly before them, constantly worship God with them, offer up secret prayer for them, and exercise a proper authority over them. There is a sort of religious gossiping which some ministers have indulged to their hurt; loitering about perpetually at the houses of their friends, and taking no delight in their own. Such conduct, in a minister and master of a family, must, of necessity, root out all family order, and, to a great degree, family worship; and, instead of endearing him to his friends, it only exposes him to their just censure. Perhaps they know not how to be so plain as to tell him of it at their own houses; but they will think the more, and speak of it, it is likely, to each other, when he is gone. I trust, my brother, that none of your domestic connexions will have to say when you are gone, "He was loose and careless in his conduct, or sour and churlish in his temper;" but rather, "He was a good man."

---

[8] 1 Corinthians 13:1–2.

2. Value this character in your private retirements. Give yourself up to "the word of God, and to prayer."[9] The apostle charged Timothy, saying, "Meditate on these things, give thyself wholly to them;" or, "be thou in them."[10] But this will never be, without a considerable share of the good man. Your heart can never be in those things which are foreign to its prevailing temper; and if your heart is not in your work, it will be a poor lifeless business indeed. We need not fear exhausting the Bible or dread a scarcity of divine subjects. If our hearts are but kept in unison with the spirit in which the Bible was written, everything we meet with there will be interesting. The more we read, the more interesting it will appear; and the more we know, the more we shall perceive there is to be known. Beware also, brother, of neglecting secret prayer. The fire of devotion will go out if it be not kept alive by an habitual dealing with Christ. Conversing with men and things may brighten our gifts and parts; but it is conversing with God that must brighten our graces. Whatever ardour we may feel in our public work, if this is wanting, things cannot be right, nor can they in such a train come to a good issue.

3. Value it in your public exercises. It is hard going on in the work of the ministry, without a good degree of spirituality; and yet, considering the present state of human nature, we are in the greatest danger of the contrary. Allow me, brother, to mention two things in particular, each of which is directly opposite to that spirit which I am attempting to recommend. One is, an assumed earnestness, or forced zeal, in the pulpit, which many weak hearers may mistake for the enjoyment of God. But though we may put on violent emotions—may smite with the hand, and stamp with the foot—if we are destitute of a genuine feeling sense of what we deliver, it will be discerned by judicious hearers, as well as by the searcher of hearts, and will not fail to create disgust. If, on the contrary, we feel and realize the

---

[9] Acts 6:4.
[10] 1 Timothy 4:15.

sentiments we deliver, emotions and actions will be the natural expressions of the heart; and this will give weight to the doctrines, exhortations, or reproofs which we inculcate; what we say will come with a kind of divine authority to the consciences, if not to the hearts of the hearers. The other is, being under the influence of low, and selfish motives in the exercise of our work. This is a temptation against which we have especial reason to watch and pray. It is right, my brother, for you to be diligent in your public work; to be instant in season and out of season; to preach the gospel not only at Thorn, but in the surrounding villages, wherever a door is opened for you: but while you are thus engaged, let it not be from motives of policy, merely to increase your auditory, but from love to Christ and the souls of your fellow sinners. It is this only that will endure reflection in a dying hour. The apostle Paul was charged by some of the Corinthian teachers with being crafty, and with having caught the Corinthians with guile; but he could say, in reply to all such insinuations, in behalf of himself and his fellow-labourers, "Our rejoicing is this, the testimony of our conscience, that in simplicity and godly sincerity, not with fleshly wisdom, but by the grace of God, we have had our conversation in the world."[11]

4. Value it in the general tenor of your behaviour. Cultivate a meek, modest, peaceful, and friendly temper. Be generous and humane. Prove by your spirit and conduct that you are a lover of all mankind. To men in general, but especially to the poor and the afflicted, be pitiful, be courteous. It is this, my brother, that will recommend the gospel you proclaim. Without this, could you preach with the eloquence of an angel, you may expect that no good end will be answered.

5. Prize the character of the good man above worldly greatness. It is not sinful for a minister, any more than another man, to possess property; but to aspire after it is unworthy of his sacred character.

---

[11] 2 Corinthians 1:12.

Greatness, unaccompanied with goodness, is valued as nothing by the great God. Kings and emperors, where that is wanting, are but great "beasts, horned beasts," pushing one at another. When Sennacherib vaunted against the church of God, that he would "enter the forest of her Carmel, and cut down her tall cedars,"[12] the daughter of Zion is commanded to despise him. God speaks of him as we should speak of a buffalo, or even of an ass: "I will put my hook in thy nose, and my bridle in thy lips, and I will turn thee back by the way by which thou camest."[13] Outward greatness, when accompanied with goodness, may be a great blessing; yet, even then, it is the latter, and not the former, that denominates the true worth of a character. Once more,

5. Value it above mental greatness, or greatness in gifts and parts. It is not wrong to cultivate gifts; on the contrary, it is our duty so to do. But, desirable as these are, they are not to be compared with goodness. "Covet earnestly the best gifts," says the apostle, "and yet show I unto you a more excellent way;"[14] viz, charity, or love. If we improve in gifts and not in grace, to say the least, it will be useless, and perhaps dangerous, both to ourselves and others. To improve in gifts, that we may be the better able to discharge our work, is laudable; but if it be for the sake of popular applause, we may expect a blast. Hundreds of ministers have been ruined by indulging a thirst for the character of the great man, while they have neglected the far superior character of the good man.

Another part of the character of Barnabas was that,

II. He was full of the Holy Spirit. The Holy Spirit sometimes denotes his extraordinary gifts, as in Acts 19, where the apostle Paul put the question to some believers in Christ whether they had received the Holy Spirit; but here it signifies his indwelling and

---

[12] Isaiah 37:24.
[13] 2 Kings 19:28; Isaiah 37:29.
[14] 1 Corinthians 12:31.

ordinary operations, or what is elsewhere called "an unction from the Holy One."[15] This, though more common than the other, is far more excellent. Its fruits, though less brilliant, are abundantly the most valuable. To be able to surmount a difficulty by Christian patience is a greater thing in the sight of God than to remove a mountain. Every work of God bears some mark of Godhead, even a thistle, or a nettle; but there are some of his works which bear a peculiar likeness to his holy moral character: such were the minds of men and angels in their original state. This will serve to illustrate the subject in hand. The extraordinary gifts of the Holy Spirit are a communication of his power; but in his dwelling in the saints, and the ordinary operations of his grace, he communicates his own holy nature; and this it was of which Barnabas was full. To be full of the Holy Spirit is to be full of the dove, as I may say; or full of those fruits of the Spirit mentioned by the apostle to the Galatians; namely, "love, joy, peace, long-suffering, gentleness, goodness."[16]

To be sure, the term full is not here to be understood in an unlimited sense; not in so ample a sense as when it is applied to Christ. He was filled with the Spirit without measure, but we in measure. The word is doubtless to be understood in a comparative sense and denotes as much as that he was habitually under his holy influence. A person that is greatly under the influence of the love of this world is said to be drunken with its cares or pleasures. In allusion to something like this, the apostle exhorts that we "be not drunken with wine, wherein is excess; but filled with the Spirit."[17] The word "filled," here, is very expressive; it denotes, I apprehend, being overcome, as it were, with the holy influences and fruits of the blessed Spirit. How necessary is all this, my brother, in your work! Oh, how necessary is "an unction from the Holy One!"

---

[15] 1 John 2:20.
[16] Galatians 5:22.
[17] Ephesians 5:18.

1. It is this that will enable you to enter into the spirit of the gospel and preserve you from destructive errors concerning it. Those who have an unction from the Holy One are said to "know all things; and the anointing which they have received abideth in them, and they need not that any man teach them, but as the same anointing teacheth them all things, and is truth, and is no lie."[18] We shall naturally fall in with the dictates of that spirit of which we are full. It is for want of this, in a great measure, that the Scriptures appear strange, and foreign, and difficult to be understood. He that is full of the Holy Spirit has the contents of the Bible written, as I may say, upon his heart; and thus its sacred pages are easy to be understood, as "wisdom is easy to him that understandeth."[19]

It is no breach of charity to say that if the professors of Christianity had more of the Holy Spirit of God in their hearts, there would be a greater harmony among them respecting the great truths which he has revealed. The rejection of such doctrines as the exceeding sinfulness of sin, the total depravity of mankind, the proper deity and atonement of Christ, justification by faith in his name, the freeness and sovereignty of grace, and the agency of the Holy Spirit, may easily be accounted for upon this principle. If we are destitute of the Holy Spirit, we are blind to the loveliness of the divine character, and destitute of any true love to God in our hearts; and if destitute of this, we shall not be able to see the reasonableness of that law which requires love to him with all the heart; and then, of course, we shall think lightly of the nature of those offences committed against him; we shall be naturally disposed to palliate and excuse our want of love to him, yea, and even our positive violations of his law; it will seem hard, very hard indeed, for such little things as these to be punished with everlasting destruction.

---

[18] 1 John 2:27.
[19] Proverbs 14:6.

And now, all this admitted, we shall naturally be blind to the necessity and glory of salvation by Jesus Christ. If sin is so trifling an affair, it will seem a strange and incredible thing that God should become incarnate to atone for it; and hence we shall be very easily persuaded to consider Christ as only a good man, who came into the world to set us a good example; or, at least, that he is not equal with the Father. The freeness and sovereignty of grace also, together with justification by imputed righteousness, will be a very strange sound in our ears. Like the Jews, we shall "go about to establish our own righteousness and shall not submit to the righteousness of God." It will seem equally strange and incredible to be told that we are by nature utterly unfit for the kingdom of God; that, therefore, we must be born again; that we are so bad that we cannot even come to Christ for life, except the Father draw us; yea, and that our best doings, after all, are unworthy of God's notice. It will be no wonder if, instead of receiving these unwelcome and humiliating doctrines, we should coincide with those writers and preachers who think more favourably of our condition, and the condition of the world at large; who either deny eternal punishment to exist, or represent men in general as being in little or no danger of it. And having avowed these sentiments, it will then become necessary to compliment their abettors (including ourselves in the number) as persons of a more rational and liberal way of thinking than other people.

My dear brother, of all things, be this your prayer, "Take not thy Holy Spirit from me!"[20] If once we sink into such a way of performing our public work as not to depend on his enlightening and enlivening influences, we may go on, and probably shall go on, from one degree of evil to another. Knowing how to account for the operations of our own minds, without imputing them to a divine agency, we shall be inclined, in this manner, to account for the operations in the

---

[20] Psalm 51:11.

mind of others; and so, with numbers in the present age, may soon call in question even "whether there be any Holy Spirit."[21]

2. Being full of the Holy Spirit will give a holy tincture to your meditation and preaching. There is such a thing as the mind being habitually under the influence of divine things, and retaining so much of a savour of Christ as that divine truths shall be viewed and expressed, as I may say, in their own language. Spiritual things will be spiritually discerned, and if spiritually discerned, will be spiritually communicated. There is more in our manner of thinking and speaking upon divine truth than perhaps, at first sight, we are aware of. A great part of the phraseology of Scripture is by some accounted unfit to be addressed to a modern ear; and is, on this account, to a great degree laid aside, even by those who profess to be satisfied with the sentiments. Whatever may be said in defense of this practice, in a very few instances, such as those where words in a translation are become obsolete, or convey a different idea from what they did at the time of being translated, I am satisfied the practice in general is very pernicious. There are many sermons that cannot fairly be charged with untruth, which yet have a tendency to lead off the mind from the simplicity of the gospel.

If such Scripture terms, for instance, as "holiness, godliness, grace, believers, saints, communion with God," etc., should be thrown aside as savouring too much of cant and enthusiasm, and such terms as morality, virtue, religion, good men, happiness of mind, etc., substituted in their room, it will have an amazing effect upon the hearers. If such preaching is the gospel, it is the gospel heathenized, and will tend to heathenize the minds of those who deal in it. I do not mean to object to the use of these latter terms, in their place; they are some of them Scriptural terms: what I object to is putting them in the place of others, when discoursing upon evangelical subjects. To be sure, there is a way of handling divine subjects

---

[21] Acts 19:2.

after this sort that is very clever and very ingenious; and a minister of such a stamp may commend himself, by his ingenuity, to many hearers: but, after all, God's truths are never so acceptable and savoury to a gracious heart as when clothed in their own native phraseology. The more you are filled, my brother, with an unction from the Holy One, the greater relish you will possess for that savoury manner of conveying truth which is so plentifully exemplified in the Holy Scriptures. Further,

3. It is this that will make the doctrines you preach, and the duties you inculcate, seem fitted in your lips. I allude to a saying of the wise man: "The words of the wise are pleasant, if thou keep them within thee; they shall withal be fitted in thy lips."[22] It is expected that there should be an agreement between the character of the speaker and the things which are spoken. "Excellent speech becometh not a fool."[23] Exhortations to holiness come with an ill grace from the lips of one who indulges himself in iniquity. The opposite of this is what I mean by the doctrines and duties of religion being fitted in your lips. It is this that will make your face shine, when you come forth in your public labours, like the face of Moses when he had been conversing with God in the holy mount.

4. It is this that will give a spiritual savour to your conversation in your visits to your friends. Though religious visits may be abused; yet you know, brother, the necessity there is for them, if you would ascertain the spiritual condition of those to whom you preach. There are many faults also that you may discover in individuals which it would be unhandsome, as well as unfriendly, to expose in a pointed manner in the pulpit, which nevertheless ought not to be passed by unnoticed. Here is work for your private visits; and, in proportion as you are filled with the Holy Spirit, you will possess a spirit of love and faithfulness, which is absolutely necessary to successful reproof.

---

[22] Proverbs 22:18.
[23] Proverbs 17:7.

It is in our private visits also that we can be free with our people, and they with us. Questions may be asked and answered, difficulties solved, and the concerns of the soul discussed. Paul taught the Ephesians, not only publicly, but "from house to house."[24] Now it is being full of the Holy Spirit that will give a spiritual savour to all this conversation. It will be as the holy anointing oil on Aaron's garments, which diffused a savour on all around him.

5. This will also teach you how you ought to behave yourself in every department you are called to occupy. It will serve instead of ten thousand rules; and all rules without it will be of no account. This it is that will teach you to be of a meek, mild, peaceful, humble spirit. It will make such a spirit be natural to you. "As touching brotherly love," said the apostle to the Thessalonians, "ye need not that I write unto you, for ye yourselves are taught of God to love one another."[25]

6. In short, it is this that will denominate you the man of God. Such was Barnabas, and such, my brother, was your predecessor, whose memory is dear to many of us;[26] and such, according to all that I have heard, was his predecessor, whose memory is equally dear to many here present.[27] Each, in his day, was a burning and shining light; but they shine here no more. May you, my brother, and each of us, be followers of them, as they also were of Christ!

Another part of the character of Barnabas is,

III. He was full of faith. It may be difficult to ascertain with precision the real meaning and extent of this term; but, I should think, in this connexion it includes, at least, the three following ideas: having the mind occupied with divine sentiment; being rooted and grounded in the truth of the gospel, and daily living upon it. The first of these ideas distinguished him from those characters whose minds

---

[24] Acts 5:42.
[25] 1 Thessalonians 4:9.
[26] David Evans was the pastor of the Thorn congregation from 1781-1787.
[27] William Butfield served the Thorn congregation from 1775-1778.

QUALIFICATIONS & ENCOURAGEMENT

are void of principle; the next, from such as are always hovering upon the borders of scepticism; and the last, from those who, though they have no manner of doubts about the truth of the doctrines of the gospel, yet scarcely ever, if at all, feel their vital influence upon their hearts and lives. Let us review each of these a little more particularly.

1. His mind was well occupied, or stored, with divine sentiment. How necessary is this to a gospel minister! It is to be feared that many young men have rushed into the work of the Lord without any decided principles of their own; yea, and have not only begun in such a state of mind, but have continued so all through their lives. Alas! what can the churches expect from such characters? What can such a void produce? How can we feed others with knowledge and understanding if we ourselves are destitute of them? To say the least, such ministers will be but "unprofitable servants."[28] But this is not all; a minister that is not inured to think for himself is constantly exposed to every false sentiment, or system, that happens to be presented to him. We sometimes hear of a person changing his sentiments; and, doubtless, in many cases it is just and right he should change them: but there are cases in which that mode of speaking is very improper; for, in reality, some persons have no sentiments of their own to change; they have only changed the sentiments of some one great man for those of another.

2. He had a firm persuasion of the truth of that gospel which he preached to others. He was rooted and grounded in the gospel. The great controversy of that day was whether the gospel was true; whether Jesus was the Messiah; whether he, who so lately expired on the cross, was the Son of God; and whether his death was the way to obtain eternal life. There were great temptations for a person who should view things through a medium of sense to think otherwise. The popular opinion went against it. To the Jews it was a stumbling-block, and to the Greeks foolishness. Those who adhered to the

---

[28] Luke 17:10.

gospel, thereby exposed themselves to cruel persecutions. But Barnabas was "full of faith;" he was decidedly on the Lord's side; he "believed on the Son of God," and had the "witness" of the truth of his gospel "within himself."

Preaching the gospel is bearing a testimony for God; but we shall never be able to do this to any good purpose, if we be always hesitating and indulging a sceptical disposition. There is no need of a dogmatical, overbearing temper; but there is need of being rooted and grounded in the truths of God. "Be not carried about," said the apostle to the Hebrews, "with strange doctrines: it is a good thing that the heart be established with grace."[29] But he elsewhere condemns the character of those who are "ever learning, and never able to come to the knowledge of the truth.[30]

3. That gospel which he preached to others he himself lived upon. "The word preached," we are told, "did not profit some, because it was not mixed with faith in them that heard it."[31] This will equally hold good in the case of the preacher as of the hearer. If we mix not faith with the doctrine we deliver, it will not profit us. Whatever abilities we may possess, and of whatever use we may be made to others, unless we can say, in some sort, with the apostle John, "That which we have seen with our eyes, and looked upon, and our hands have handled of the word of life-that declare we unto you,"[32] our own souls may, notwithstanding, everlastingly perish! This is a very serious matter, and well deserves our attention as ministers. Professors in the age of Barnabas might be under greater temptations than we are to question whether Jesus was the true Messiah; but we are under greater temptations than they were of resting in a mere implicit assent to the Christian religion, without realizing and living upon its important truths.

---

[29] Hebrews 13:9.
[30] 2 Timothy 3:7.
[31] Hebrews 4:2.
[32] 1 John 1:1.

QUALIFICATIONS & ENCOURAGEMENT

The studying of divine truth as preachers rather than as Christians, or, in other words, studying it for the sake of finding out something to say to others, without so much as thinking of profiting our own souls, is a temptation to which we are more than ordinarily exposed. If we studied divine truths as Christians, our being constantly engaged in the service of God would be friendly to our growth in grace. We should be "like trees planted by the rivers of waters, that bring forth fruit in their season," and all that we did would be likely to "prosper."[33] But if we study it only as preachers, it will be the reverse. Our being conversant with the Bible will be like surgeons and soldiers being conversant with the shedding of human blood, till they lose all sensibility concerning it. I believe it is a fact that, where a preacher is wicked, he is generally the most hardened against conviction of any character whatever. Happy will it be for us if, like Barnabas, we are "full of faith" in that Saviour whom we recommend—in that gospel which it is our employment to proclaim.

IV. We now come to the last part of the subject, which is held up by way of encouragement: and much people was added unto the Lord. When our ministry is blessed to the conversion of sinners, to the bringing them off from their connexion with sin and self to a vital union with Christ; when our congregations are filled, not merely with professors of religion, but with sound believers; when such believers come forward and offer themselves willingly for communion, saying, "We will go with you, for we have heard that God is with you;"[34] then it may be said that "much people is added unto the Lord."[35] The connexion between such additions, and eminency in grace and holiness in a minister, deserves our serious attention.

I think it may be laid down as a rule, which both Scripture and experience will confirm, that eminent spirituality in a minister is

---

[33] Psalm 1:3.
[34] Zechariah 8:23.
[35] Acts 11:24.

usually attended with eminent usefulness. I do not mean to say our usefulness depends upon our spirituality, as an effect depends upon its cause; nor yet that it is always in proportion to it. God is a Sovereign; and frequently sees proper to convince us of it, in variously bestowing his blessing on the means of grace. But yet he is not wanting in giving encouragement to what he approves, wherever it is found. Our want of usefulness is often to be ascribed to our want of spirituality, much oftener than to our want of talents. God has frequently been known to succeed men of inferior abilities, when they have been eminent for holiness, while he has blasted others of much superior talents, when that quality has been wanting. Hundreds of ministers, who, on account of their gifts, have promised to be shining characters, have proved the reverse; and all owing to such things as pride, unwatchfulness, carnality, and levity.

Eminency in grace, my brother, will contribute to your success in three ways:

1. It will fire your soul with holy love to Christ and the souls of men; and such a spirit is usually attended with success. I believe you will find that, in almost all the great works which God has wrought, in any period of time, he has honoured men of this character, by making them his instruments. In the midst of a sore calamity upon the murmuring Israelites, when God was inclined to show mercy, it was by the means of his servant Aaron running with a censer of fire in his hand, and standing between the living and the dead! The great reformation that was brought about in the days of Hezekiah was by the instrumentality of a man "who wrought that which was good and right and truth before the Lord his God;" and then it follows, "and in every work that he began in the service of the house of God, and in the law, and in the commandments, to seek his God, he did it with all his heart, and prospered."[36]

---

[36] 2 Chronicles 31:20–21.

Qualifications & Encouragement

There was another great reformation in the Jewish church, about the time of their return from Babylon. One of the chief instruments in this work was Ezra, "a ready scribe in the law of his God;"[37] a man who had "prepared his heart to seek the law of the Lord, and to do it, and to teach in Israel statutes and judgments;"[38] a man who "fasted and prayed at the river Ahava,"[39] previously to his great undertaking; a man who was afterwards "sorely astonished, and in heaviness, and would eat no meat, nor drink water, but fell upon his knees, and spread out his hands unto the Lord his God, on account of the transgressions of the people."[40] Another great instrument in this work was Nehemiah, a man that devoted himself wholly to the service of God and his people, labouring night and day, and was not to be seduced by the intrigues of God's adversaries, nor yet intimidated by their threatenings; but persevered in his work till it was finished, closing his labours with this solemn prayer and appeal, "Think upon me, O my God, for good, according to all that I have done for this people."[41]

Time would fail me to speak of all the great souls, both inspired and uninspired, whom the King of kings has delighted to honour: of Paul, and Peter, and their companions; of Wickliff,[42] and Luther, and Calvin,[43] and many others at the Reformation; of Elliot,[44] and Edwards, and Brainerd, and Whitefield,[45] and hundreds more whose

---

[37] Ezra 7:6.
[38] Ezra 7:10.
[39] Ezra 8:21.
[40] Isaiah 37:32.
[41] Nehemiah 5:19.
[42] John Wycliffe (c.1330-1384) promoted the translation of the Bible into Middle English so as to undergird his program of reform of the medieval Church.
[43] Martin Luther (1483-1546) and John Calvin (1509-1564) were two central Protestant figures at the time of the Reformation.
[44] John Eliot (1604-1690) was a Puritan missionary to the Algonquian Indians in Massachusetts.
[45] Jonathan Edwards, David Brainerd (1718-1747)—an Evangelical missionary to the Delaware Indians of New Jersey—and George Whitefield (1714-1770) were three eminent Evangelicals of the long eighteenth century. On Edwards, see above, page 2.

names are held in deserved esteem in the church of God. These were men of God; men who had great grace, as well as gifts; whose hearts burned in love to Christ and the souls of men. They looked upon their hearers as their Lord had done upon Jerusalem and wept over them. In this manner they delivered their messages; "and much people were added unto the Lord."[46]

2. Eminency in grace will direct your ends to the glory of God, and the welfare of men's souls; and where this is the case, it is usually attended with a blessing. These are ends which God himself pursues; and if we pursue the same, we are "labourers together with God,"[47] and may hope for his blessing to attend our labours; but if we pursue separate and selfish ends, we walk contrary to God, and may expect God to walk contrary to us. Whatever apparent success may attend the labours of a man whose ends are evil, all is to be suspected; either the success is not genuine, or, if it be, it is not in a way of blessing upon him, nor shall it turn out, at last, to his account. It must be an inexpressible satisfaction, brother, to be able to say as the primitive ministers and apostles did: "James, a servant of God ... Paul, a servant of Jesus Christ ... We seek not yours, but you."[48]

3. Eminency in grace will enable you to bear prosperity in your ministry without being lifted up with it; and so contribute towards it. It is written of Christ, in prophecy, "He shall build the temple of the Lord, and shall bear the glory."[49] He does bear it indeed; but to bear glory without being elated is no easy thing for us. I am often afraid lest this should be one considerable reason why most of us have no more real success in our work than we have; perhaps it is not safe for us to be much owned of God; perhaps we have not grace enough to bear prosperity.

---

[46] Acts 11:24.
[47] 1 Corinthians 3:9.
[48] James 1:1; Romans 1:1; 2 Corinthians 12:14.
[49] Zechariah 6:13.

Qualifications & Encouragement

My dear brother, permit me to conclude with a word or two of serious advice. First, "Watch over your own soul, as well as the souls of your people."[50] Do not forget that ministers are peculiarly liable, while they keep the vineyard of others, to neglect their own. Further, "Know your own weakness, and depend upon Christ's all-sufficiency."[51] Your work is great, your trials may be many; but let not your heart be discouraged. Remember what was said to the apostle Paul, "My grace is sufficient for thee, my strength is made perfect in weakness,"[52] and the reflection which he makes upon it, "When I am weak, then am I strong."[53]

Finally, be often looking to the end of your course, and viewing yourself as giving an account of your stewardship. We must all appear before the judgment-seat of Christ, and give account of the deeds done in the body. Perhaps there is no thought more solemn than this, more suitable to be kept in view in all our undertakings, more awakening in a thoughtless hour, or more cheering to an upright heart.

I have only to request, my dear brother, that you will excuse the freedom of this plain address. I have not spoken so much to instruct you in things which you know not, as to remind and impress you with things which you already know. The Lord bless you, and grant that the solemnities of this day may ever be remembered with satisfaction, both by you and your people!

---

[50] Hebrews 13:17.
[51] 2 Corinthians 12:9.
[52] 2 Corinthians 12:9.
[53] 2 Corinthians 12:10.

Questions

1. What is the importance of examples from Fuller's perspective? How can an example drawn from Scripture be helpful to a young minister like Robert Fawkner?
2. What kind of man was Barnabas? Why is he a good example?
3. What does the epithet "good" in Acts 11:24 mean according to Fuller?
4. How does being a good man work itself out in: (a) the home; (b) one's personal life; (c) one's public life as a minister; and (d) the "general tenor of your behavior"?
5. What is key to making sure "the fire of devotion" does not go out?
6. What does the indwelling of the Holy Spirit entail? According to Fuller, what is meant by the metaphor "full of the Holy Spirit"?
7. What results flow from being filled with the Holy Spirit?
8. Write a small paragraph on the phrase "if we are destitute of the Holy Spirit, we are blind to the loveliness of the divine character."
9. Given the reality of the perseverance of the believer, can a Christian pray David's prayer, "Take not thy Holy Spirit"? If so, why? If not, why not?
10. What is one of the marks of Fuller's day?
11. Read this passage and detail how it explains what Fuller means when he says, "Being full of the Holy Spirit will give a holy tincture to your meditation and preaching."
12. a. How will being filled with the Holy Spirit impact one's relationship with one's congregation?
    b. What key role of pastoral ministry will being filled with the Spirit impact?

Qualifications & Encouragement

    c. What is significant about the way that Fuller refers to the members of the congregation whom the minister will visit?
13. How will experiencing the fullness of the Holy Spirit affect one's character?
14. What three possible meanings does Fuller discern in the phrase "full of faith"?
15. What was "the great controversy" of Paul's day?
16. What "rule" does "Scripture and experience ... confirm"? Discuss Fuller's rule. Do you agree with Fuller? Why or why not?
17. What three distinguishing marks of eminent spirituality or "eminency in grace" does Fuller identify?
18. What three pieces of "serious advice" close this sermon? Is there one of these that is particularly apropos to your life? Explain.

Robert Robinson

4
Strictures on Some of the Leading Sentiments of Mr. R. Robinson: Letter III: On Liberty[1] (1788?)

Introduction

Robert Robinson (1735–1790) had been converted under the ministry of the Anglican evangelist George Whitefield (1714–1770) and, after a short career as a Methodist preacher, he became a Particular Baptist and went on to build a thriving work at St. Andrew's Street Baptist Church, Cambridge, where he became known as one of the finest colloquial preachers in England. Towards the end of his life, though, he became increasingly critical of both the Calvinism and Trinitarian doctrine of his denominational community. He is remembered for his marvellous hymn, "Come, Thou Fount of every blessing."[2] When Fuller was contemplating making the move from Soham to Kettering in the early 1780s, he consulted Robinson for advice. By the close of that decade, though, Robinson's theological drift prompted Fuller to write this critical reflection that formed a

---

[1] From *The Complete Works of the Rev. Andrew Fuller*, ed. Joseph Belcher (1845, Harrisonburg, VA: Sprinkle Publications, 1988), *Works*, III, 597–601.

On the life of Robert Robinson, see Graham W. Hughes, *With Freedom Fired: The Story of Robert Robinson Cambridge Nonconformist* (London: Carey Kingsgate Press, 1955); L.G. Champion, "Robert Robinson: A Pastor In Cambridge," *The Baptist Quarterly* 31 (1985–1986): 241–246; Len Addicott, "Introduction" to his, L.G. Champion, and K.A.C. Parsons, ed., *Church Book: St Andrew's Street Baptist Church, Cambridge 1720-1832* ([London]: Baptist Historical Society, 1991), viii–xviii.

[2] The oldest surviving publication of this hymn is in *A Collection of Hymns for the Use of the Church of Christ: Meeting in Angel-Alley* (London, 1759). It was first published probably as a broadsheet, of which no known exemplars survive. See details at Hymnology Archive (https://www.hymnologyarchive.com/come-thou-fount; accessed August 13, 2020).

part of a collection of six letters on different aspects of Robinson's thought.

On Liberty
My dear friend,

It has long been the opinion of many persons, who are by no means unfriendly to liberty, that Mr. Robinson's notions of it are licentious and extravagant; and in this opinion I cannot help concurring.

Liberty seems to consist in the power of acting without control or impediment. But the term, being relative, must be understood in relation to the different objects which are supposed to be impediments.

Some have defined liberty as the power of doing what we please; and this definition will doubtless apply to every kind of liberty except moral. But moral liberty, which is of greater importance than any other kind of liberty, does not consist in this. Though we do as we please in the exercise of moral liberty, this is not that by which it is distinguished from other things; no, not from moral slavery itself. Moral slavery is not that state in which a person is compelled to act against his will; but rather a state in which he is impelled to act against his conscience. A person may have the power of doing what he pleases, to the greatest possible degree, and yet be totally destitute of moral liberty, being a perfect slave to his own appetites.

Some persons, perhaps justly, have classed liberty under four kinds—physical, moral, civil, and religious. Physical liberty is the power of doing what we please without any natural restraints or impediments. If our actions are not the free result of our choice, that is, if they are directed or impeded by an influence contrary to our will, we are destitute of this liberty. Moral liberty is the power of doing what is right, without being impeded by sinful dispositions or passions. A libertine, with all his boasted freedom, is here a perfect slave. "While they promise themselves liberty, they themselves are the servants of corruption; for of whom a man is overcome, of the same is he brought in bondage." Civil liberty, as it is commonly understood in Britain, is freedom from all fear of punishment contrary to law, and from subjection to any laws but those to which a man himself, by his representatives, gives consent. Religious liberty is the power of forming our religious sentiments, and conducting our religious worship, agreeably to the dictates of our consciences, without being liable to civil penalties.

Now, suppose Mr. R.'s notions of civil and religious liberty be just, yet surely he makes, if not too much of these, yet too little of that which is of far greater importance—moral liberty. This is the liberty of which the Scriptures chiefly speak; this is the glorious liberty of the gospel. This is that of which every unregenerate man is destitute, being a slave to sin and Satan. This is the liberty with which the Son makes us free; without which all other liberty is but a shadow and an empty boast. This is implied in the reply of our Lord to the boasting Jews, who said they were never in bondage to any man: "If the Son make you free, then are ye free indeed."[3] It is allowed, indeed, that religious liberty, or a freedom to think and act according to our consciences, without fear, is of great value, and perhaps none of us prize it sufficiently; but what is this to moral liberty? Suppose a man liberated from the tyranny of sin and Satan, and deprived of all religious and civil liberty, groaning under the yoke of powerful persecution, would he not be in an unspeakably better situation than another man, possessed of all the liberty he desired, whose soul was enslaved to sin?

Is it not strange, then, that whenever Mr. R. finds the term liberty in the New Testament he should reduce it to a simple liberty of doing as we please! And is it not passing strange that "the glorious liberty of the sons of God"[4] should be thus explained! Mr. R., having given us several quotations on the text from Greek and Latin writers, sums

---

[3] John 8:36.
[4] Romans 8:21.

up the whole in English, by adding,

> The amount, then, is this: The heathens expected some great revolution to be brought about by some extraordinary person about St. Paul's time. St. Paul was well acquainted with their opinion: it is natural, therefore, to suppose that the apostle would speak on this article and direct the eyes of the pagans to Jesus Christ. The passage is capable of such a meaning, and it is highly probable that this is the sense of it. The Gentiles are earnestly looking for such a liberty as the gospel proposes to mankind.[5]

"The question is," continues Mr. R., "what liberty the gospel does bestow on mankind." Very good; and now let us see what his "glorious liberty of the sons of God" amounts to. "In days of yore," says he, "divines were not ashamed to affirm that liberty of judging and determining matters of faith and conscience was a prerogative of the papal tiara" and so on; a long story of this kind, for four or five columns, reducing "the glorious liberty of the sons of God" to a mere liberty of "judging and determining for ourselves in matters of faith and conscience"[6]: a freedom from the control of creeds and systems, as though it did not signify what we imbibed so that we acted freely. Suppose this freedom were included, yet surely it is not the whole of the meaning. Probably the apostle alluded especially to the redemption of the bodies of believers at the resurrection. But if Mr. R. were right in applying the passage to the Gentile world, surely he might have conceived of a more glorious liberty than that of thinking and

---

[5] Jean Claude, *An Essay on the Composition of a Sermon*, trans. and annotated Robert Robinson (Cambridge: Francis Hodson, 1779), II, 62. In addition to this translation of a notable homiletical work, Robinson has added copious annotations. Fuller's disagreement is with the latter. He had a high view of Claude's work. See Andrew Fuller, "Essay on the Composition of a Sermon" in *The Preacher: or Sketches of Original Sermons, chiefly selected from the Manuscripts of Two Eminent Divines of the Last Century, for the Use of Lay Preachers and Young Ministers* (Philadelphia, PA: J. Whetham, 1838), 25

[6] Claude, *Composition of a Sermon*, II, 62.

acting for ourselves—a moral liberty—a freedom from the bondage of sin and Satan, particularly from the slavery of idolatry and superstition. This were a liberty worthwhile for the Son of God to come from heaven to bestow.

Mr. Robinson may be right in censuring the bishops for "sacrificing Christianity to save episcopacy;" but let him beware of undervaluing moral liberty for the sake of that of which he is so tenacious, of an inferior kind. Christianity is of greater importance than nonconformity. A remark of Mr. Whitefield, when he had attended one of the synods of Scotland, and had heard one of the associate presbytery preach, may not be inappropriate. "The good man," says he, "so spent himself in talking against prelacy, the *Common Prayer Book*, the surplice, the rose in the hat, and such-like externals, that when he came to the latter part of his subject, to invite poor sinners to Jesus Christ, his breath was so gone that he could scarce be heard." This passage Mr. R. introduces into his arcana with great approbation, and adds, "This will always be the case: that learning, eloquence, strength, and zeal, which should be spent in enforcing 'the weightier matters of the law, judgment, mercy, and faith,'[7] will be unprofitably wasted on 'the tithing of mint, anise, and cummin' on discarding or defending a bow to the east, or a rose in the hat."[8] How far this describes Mr. R.'s subsequent conduct, I leave you to judge.

But not only has he neglected weightier things in defending those of inferior importance, but it appears to me that his notions of liberty are latitudinarian, unscriptural, and unreasonable.

Though, in regard to men, we are at liberty to act and think as we please in religion, this is not true in regard to God. He requires us to believe the truth, as well as to obey his commands. He has given us

---

[7] Matthew 23:23.
[8] Robert Robinson, *Arcana: In VIII. Letters to a Friend* (London: J. Lepard and J. Buckland, 1782), 109.

a rule of faith, as well as of practice, and requires us to think and act according to it; and, moreover, it is at our peril that we allow ourselves in the contrary. This, however, is a distinction which I never knew Mr. R. to have made; though I could scarcely have thought he would have avowed the contrary, had he not told me in conversation that no man was bound to believe the gospel, that their only duty was to examine it, and that to make it their duty to believe, as well as to examine, would destroy their liberty, and render their errors criminal! But what can be made of such a liberty as this, unless it be a divine right to do wrong? This Mr. R. ridicules in politics:[9] is it not a pity he should retain it in divinity?

Further, there is a material difference between my being at liberty to believe and act in religious matters without being accountable to the civil authorities, or to any fellow creature as such; and my having a right, be my religious principles what they may, to a place in a Christian church. If I act with decorum in my civil capacity, I have a right, whatever be my religious principles, to all the benefits of civil government; but it does not therefore follow that I am entitled to the privileges of the house of God. Mr. R. blames the Church of England for not allowing avowed Socinians to continue in its service and receive its emoluments;[10] and not long since, unless I am misinformed, he declared in public company, at an ordination, that no church had a right to refuse any man communion, whether he were an Arian, a Sabellian, a Socinian, or an Antinomian, provided he was of good moral character!

If, however, this notion consist with either Scripture or common sense, I must confess myself a stranger to both. The church of God is represented as a city—a city with walls and bulwarks; a city with gates, of which they themselves have the care and keeping. It is true they are commanded to open the gates—but to whom? To the

---

[9] Claude, *Composition of a Sermon*, II, 42.
[10] Claude, *Composition of a Sermon*, II, 212.

righteous nation "who keep the truth." These, and these only, are to enter in.[11]

2. I know the objection Mr. R. would make to this; viz. "Who is to judge what is truth?" But, on this principle, we may doubt of everything, and turn sceptics at once; or else consider that to be truth which any man thinks is truth. But if it be indeed so difficult to ascertain the truth as that we must needs give over judging in that matter, and that must pass for truth which every person thinks to be such, then surely the Bible cannot be such a plain book as Mr. R. represents. Besides, we might on the same principle refrain from judging between right and wrong; for there are various opinions about these, as well as about truth and error. Suppose, for instance, a person were to apply to a Christian church for communion who approved and practised polygamy, or who should think that Scripture sanctioned concubinage, and therefore practised it; upon this principle, the church must be silent, for should they object to such practices as immoral, it might be replied, "I think they are right; and who are you that you should set us for judges of right and wrong in other men's conduct?" Mr. R. therefore need not have been so squeamish in his proposed reception of Arians and Socinians as to provide for their good moral character. Upon his principle, the want of character ought to be no objection, provided they are so abandoned in vice as to believe that evil is good, or so versed in hypocrisy as to say they believe so, whether they do or not.

I do not see how the church at Pergamos could have been blamed by the Lord Jesus for having those among them that held the doctrine of Balaam and of the Nicolaitans, unless they were authorized, and even required, to judge of right and wrong, truth and error, in relation to those whom they received as members. On Mr. R.'s principles, they might have excused themselves in some such manner as this: "Lord, we never apprehended we had anything to do in judging

---

[11] Isaiah 26:1

of the doctrines that people held who became members with us: we came together upon the liberal principles of universal toleration, and never expected to be called to account about any one's sentiments but our own, whatever we were for these." But, in reply to all such pleas as this, it is sufficient to say, "Thus saith He that hath the sharp two-edged sword, I have somewhat against thee."[12]

As to the bugbear frequently held up—that if we presume to judge in these matters we assume to ourselves infallibility, to what does it amount? On this principle all human judgment must be set aside in civil as well as in sacred things. No man, nor any set of men, can pretend to this; neither need they. It is sufficient that they act to the best of their capacity, availing themselves of all the means of information they possess. All men, undoubtedly, are fallible; it becomes them, therefore, to judge with meekness and fear; and to consider that their decisions are not final, that they must all be brought over again, and themselves be tried with them at the great assize! But does it thence follow that all human judgment must be laid aside? Surely not.

The great outcry that Mr. R. has made of our Lord's words, "Call no man master,"[13] etc., is no more to his purpose than the other. Surely it is one thing to dictate to a man what he shall believe, and persecute him if he does not; and another to require a union of principles, in order that we may unite with him in church fellowship, and have communion with him in the ordinances of Jesus Christ. As an individual, we have nothing to do with him: to his own master he standeth or falleth; and we the same. But if he propose to have Christian fellowship with us, it is right that we should inquire whether his principles so far coincide with ours as that the end proposed may be accomplished. Is there not a wide difference between my persecuting, or wishing to persecute, a deist, and refusing to unite with him

---

[12] Revelation 2:2.
[13] Matthew 23:8.

in church fellowship?

I believe also that Mr. R.'s principles are as opposed to right reason, to common sense, and to the rules of society in general, as they are to Scripture.

In large societies, the government of a nation for instance, they are obliged to be very general, and cannot maintain such a minute regularity as in societies of less extent. But even here some union of sentiment is required. Suppose a Jacobite, for example, were to insist that King George was not the rightful possessor of the throne, would he have a right to form one of his Majesty's ministry? And suppose he were to express his intention, if opportunity offered, of uniting to dethrone him, would not the government have a right to banish him the kingdom? Whether they would invariably use their right is another thing; but the right itself they would undoubtedly possess.

In smaller societies, where persons unite for the sake of obtaining certain ends, it is always expected that they should agree in certain leading principles necessary to the accomplishment of those ends. Hence, there is scarcely a society formed without articles, testifying the agreement of the members in certain fundamental particulars. Suppose, for example, a common club, united for the purpose of assisting each other in time of affliction. It is supposed to be a leading principle of such a society, that the lesser number of members should, in all matters of debate, submit to the greater; and another that a certain sum of money should be paid by each member at certain times. Now, just suppose any one member should dissent from the rules; common sense suggests the necessity of his being convinced or excluded. But it seems a Christian society has not the authority of a common club!

It cannot be difficult to prove that a union of faith respecting the proper deity of the Great Author of our religion, and the object of our worship, is of quite as much importance in religious society as any of the above in civil society. Surely, the dethroning of the Son of

God, by the denial of his essential deity, cannot be less pernicious in the gospel dispensation, than the denial of his Majesty's authority, and the endeavour to dethrone him, would be in these realms.

Some of the grand ends of Christian society are, unitedly to worship God, to devote ourselves to the blessed Trinity by Christian baptism, and to acknowledge the atonement made by the Redeemer, by a participation of the ordinance of the Lord's supper. But what union could there be in worship where the object worshiped is not the same—where one party believes the other to be an idolater, and the other believes him to be a degrader of him who is "over all, God, blessed for ever?"[14] What fellowship could there be in the Lord's supper, for instance (not to mention baptism), where one party thought sin to be an infinite evil—that they, being the subjects of it, deserved an infinite curse—that no atonement could be made but by an infinite sacrifice—that the sacrifice of Christ was such, and an instance of infinite grace and love—and that the design of the sacred supper is to revive in our minds these affecting truths; and where the other party believed none of these things—had no conception that sin was so great an evil as to deserve infinite punishment, or to need an infinite atonement—that, in fact, they are not such great sinners as to need not only a Saviour, but a great one? That which is to the one "the glorious gospel of the blessed God"[15] is to the other foolishness, and an insult, forsooth, upon his dignity!

If ever any professed Christians differed in the essentials of religion, Calvinists and Socinians do. I wish to conduct myself towards a Socinian no otherwise than I believe a Socinian ought to conduct himself towards me, on the supposition that I am in error. Dr. Priestley acts more consistently, and more like an honest man, than Mr. R.[16] He denies the propriety of Unitarians and Trinitarians uniting

---

[14] Romans 9:5.
[15] 1 Timothy 1:11.
[16] Joseph Priestley (1733–1804) was an outspoken advocate of Socinianism.

together in divine worship, and exhorts all of the former class to form separate societies. This I cordially approve; for verily, whatever esteem we may entertain for each other as men, in religion there can be no harmony. Either we are a company of idolaters, or they are enemies to the gospel—rendering the cross of Christ of none effect. Either they are unbelievers, or we are at least as bad—rendering to a creature that homage which is due only to the Creator; and, in either case, a union is the last degree of absurdity.

Whatever then, my dear friend, Mr. R. or anyone else may suggest, under the specious pretence of liberality of sentiment, I trust you and I shall ever give heed to the better reasonings of an inspired apostle:

> What fellowship hath righteousness with unrighteousness? and what communion hath light with darkness? and what concord hath Christ with Belial? and what part hath he that believeth with an infidel? Be ye not unequally yoked together with unbelievers.[17]

---

[17] 2 Corinthians 6:14–17.

Questions

1. How many kinds of liberty does Fuller identify and how are they to be defined?
2. Why does Fuller believe that moral liberty is the most important type of freedom?
3. Why does Fuller believe that "we are at liberty to act and think as we please in religion" with regard to men, but not God? What does Robert Robinson believe with regard to this?
4. What does this letter tell you about Fuller's understanding of the local church?
5. How does Fuller answer the accusation that "if we presume to judge in these matters we assume to ourselves infallibility"? How does Fuller envisage Robinson responding to this? What surrejoinder does Fuller make?
6. How does Fuller demonstrate that Robinson's perspective is inimical "to right reason, to common sense, and to the rules of society in general"?
7. What takes place in baptism? And at the Lord's Table?
8. What is the Gospel according to pages 68–69?

William Vidler

5
Letter I to William Vidler
On the Doctrine of Universal Salvation[1]
(1793)

Introduction
Raised in the Church of England, William Vidler (1758-1816) initially embraced Calvinist Independency in the 1770s and between 1777 and 1780 led an Independent congregation at Battle, Sussex, his birthplace, as it grew from 15 to 150 members. In 1780, though, Vidler came to Particular Baptist convictions and was baptized at Rye Baptist Church in the spring of that year.[2] A majority of the Independent congregation re-organized themselves under his leadership as a Particular Baptist church and in 1790 built a new chapel with an indebtedness of £700. Seeking to raise funds to eliminate this debt, Vidler made a tour of a number of Baptist churches in May of 1791. On these peregrinations he met both Arminians and Universalists, who challenged his thinking on matters both soteriological and eschatological. And by 1792 he had become a Universalist, which led to a division in his congregation after a huge debate took place that year on Christmas Day and New Year's Eve. A large majority remained with Vidler as Universalists, but 15 people left the church and continued as Particular Baptists. In later years Vidler moved to London as the assistant pastor of a Universalist congregation.

Vidler had met Fuller on his travels, and Fuller winsomely, though without compromise, sought to win him back to a biblical

---

[1] From Andrew Fuller, *Letters to Mr. Vidler, On the Doctrine of Universal Salvation* (Clipstone: J.W. Morris, 1802), 5-10.
[2] A. Hedley Brown, *The Rye Baptists From 1750 to 1904* (Rye: Deacon's Printing and Publishing Works, [1904]), 17.

position on the destiny of the impenitent. It was not long, though, before this drift into heterodoxy led Vidler to question other key doctrines. And by the early 1800s he had come to deny Christ's essential deity and thus to embrace Unitarianism.[3]

The text reproduced here is the first of a series of letters that Fuller sent to Vidler, which he later published as *Letters to Mr. Vidler, On the Doctrine of Universal Salvation* (1802). They well reveal the winsome nature of Fuller's apologetics, and the fact that it was love that motivated his response to Vidler.

On the Doctrine of Universal Salvation

February 14, 1793

My dear friend,

It has afforded me some painful concern to hear of your having embraced the scheme of universal salvation. When you were at Kettering, you appeared to me to be of a speculative disposition. I have long thought such a turn of mind to be very advantageous, or very dangerous. Persons of this description either make great advances in truth, or fall into great errors. I cannot, in this letter, enter deeply into the controversy; nor is there any necessity for it, as I am told that Dr. Edwards's *Answer to Dr. Chauncey* is in your hands.[4] I earnestly wish you may read that piece with care, impartiality, and openness to conviction. I think you ought to have read it before you advanced your change of sentiment; and I greatly wish you had, for

---

[3] Brian A. Packer, *Planted By Vidler. Northiam Unitarian Chapel: A History* (Tenterden, Kent, 1988), 1-8; Keith Foord, "William Vidler—a Peculiar Clergyman" (Unpublished essay, 2017).

[4] Jonathan Edwards, Jr., *The Salvation of All Men Strictly Examined; and the Endless Punishment of those who Die Impenitent, Argued and Defended against the Objections and Reasonings of the late Rev. Doctor Chauncy, of Boston*, in his book entitled *The Salvation of All Men* (New Haven, CT: A. Morse, 1790). Jonathan Edwards, Jr. was the second son of Fuller's theological hero, Jonathan Edwards, and a leading figure of the theological movement that came be called the "New Divinity."

Charles Chauncey (1705-1787) was a Boston Congregationalist minister who came to oppose the Great Awakening and promote both Unitarianism and Universalism.

Doctrine of Universal Salvation

though I do not question your openness to conviction, any more than that of any other person in your situation, yet I know something of what is in man. I know it is a very rare thing, when we have once openly disavowed a sentiment, to return to it, and openly avow it again. There are many instances of people changing their principles, and there may have been instances of the other, but I do not recollect any. False shame, supported by mistaken pride, forms here a very powerful temptation. The dread of being accused of versatility and indecision insensibly obtains such a dominion over the mind as to blind it to one side of the argument, and to give efficacy to everything that looks like an argument, or the shadow of an argument, on the other.

It is certainly a very serious matter that we do not err in our ministrations. Error in a minister may affect the eternal welfare of many. I hope I may presume upon the friendliness of your temper, while I expostulate with you upon the subject. I will not be tedious to you; but let me intreat you to consider the following things:

First: whether your change of sentiment has not arisen from an idea of endless punishment being in itself unjust. If it has, consider whether this does not arise from diminutive notions of the evil of sin; whether you be not too much infected by sin yourself to be a proper judge of its demerit. A company of criminals would be very improper judges of the equity and goodness of a law which condemns them. [Consider] whether you do not hold a principle from which it will follow, that millions will be finally happy who will not be indebted to either the grace of God or the death of Christ for their happiness; and consequently, must have a heaven to themselves, not being able to join with those who ascribe theirs to God and the Lamb. For if endless misery be unjust, exemption from it must be the sinner's right, and can never be attributed to mercy; neither could a mediator be needed to induce a righteous God to liberate the sinner, when he had suffered his full desert. In fine, consider whether you do not contradict your own experience. I think you have told me of your great distress of soul, arising from a consciousness of your deserving to be cast out of God's favour, and banished forever from his presence. Can you now say that you did not deserve this? Do you not deserve it still? If you do, why not others?

Secondly, consider whether the genius of the sentiment in question be not opposite to that of every other sentiment in the Bible. The whole tenor of Scripture saith, "to the righteous, it shall be well with him; and to the wicked, it shall be ill with him."[5] But universal salvation saith, not only to the righteous, but to the wicked, it shall be well at last with him. Do consider whether you can find any one Scripture truth that resembles it in this respect. What doctrine, besides this, can you find in the Bible that affords encouragement to a sinner going on still in his trespasses, and which furnishes ground for hope and joy, even supposing him to persevere in sin till death? Instead of siding with God against a wicked world, as a servant of God ought to do, is not this siding with a wicked world against God, and encouraging them to believe, what they are apt enough to believe without encouragement, that they "shall have peace, though they add drunkenness to thirst!"[6] "Woe is me," said an apostle, "if I preach not the gospel!"[7] "If an angel from heaven preach any other gospel," he is declared to be "accursed!"[8] Do seriously consider whether the doctrine of universal salvation will not render your preaching "another gospel." The gospel of Christ is good tidings to the meek, healing to the brokenhearted, and comfort to them that mourn; but must not yours be good tidings to the proud and impenitent, and comfort to those whom the Scripture declares under condemnation and the curse? The gospel of Christ is a system of holiness, a system entirely opposite to every vicious bias of the human

---

[5] Isaiah 3:10–11.
[6] See Deuteronomy 29:19.
[7] 1 Corinthians 9:16.
[8] Galatians 1:9.

heart, a system, therefore, which no unrenewed heart embraces. "He that believeth that Jesus is the Christ is born of God."[9] But the good news which you must publish requires no change of heart that it may be embraced, being just suited to the wishes of an abandoned mind.

Thirdly, consider whether your ministrations, on this principle, will not savour of his who taught our first parents, "Ye shall not surely die."[10] If you should raise the hopes of the ungodly part of your audience, that, though they should live and die in their filthiness, yet they shall not be filthy still; though they go down to the pit, yet it shall not prove bottomless; though the worm may prey upon them, yet, at some period or other, it shall die; and though they may have to encounter devouring fire, yet they shall not dwell in everlasting burnings. If, I say, you should raise such hopes, and if all at last should prove a deception, think how you will be able to look them in the face another day. And, what is still more, how you will be able to look him in the face who hath charged you to be "free from the blood of all men"[11] and to "say unto the wicked, it shall be ill with him; for the reward of his hands shall be given him!"[12]

My dear friend, do not take it unkindly. My soul is grieved for you, and for the souls of many around you. How are you as to peace of mind and communion with God? Beware of the whirlpool of Socinianism.[13] From what I understand of the nature and tendency of your principles, it appears to me you are already within the influence of its destructive stream. All who hold this sentiment, I know, are not Socinians; but there are few, if any, Socinians who do not hold this sentiment, which is certainly of a piece with their whole system.

---

[9] 1 John 5:1.
[10] Genesis 3:4.
[11] See Acts 20:26.
[12] Isaiah 3:11.
[13] Socinianism, the fastest-growing heterodoxy of the late eighteenth century, proposed a Unitarian vision of the Godhead and rejected the deity of Christ and the Holy Spirit.

Reading Andrew Fuller

It would greatly rejoice my heart to be able to acknowledge you, as heretofore, my brother and fellow labourer in the gospel of Jesus Christ. Do let me hear from you, and believe me to be

Yours, etc., A. F.

Questions

1. What dangers does Fuller see in changing one's sentiments with regard to religious matters?
2. Why is it a matter of much concern when a minister or pastor embraces theological error?
3. What does Fuller identify as a problem with the view that endless punishment is unjust?
4. Does the rejection of endless punishment accord with the Scriptures? Is Fuller correct? Why or why not?
5. What do you sense is the overall tone of Fuller's approach to Vidler?

Cyprian of Carthage, whom Fuller would have called a "primitive disciple" (a sixteenth-century print)

6
Why Christians in the Present Day Possess Less Joy Than the Primitive Disciples[1]
(1795)

Introduction

On no less than nine occasions, Andrew Fuller had the privilege of writing the annual circular letter for the Northamptonshire Association. This one was penned during the turbulent and troubling 1790s when revolution and war stalked Europe.

Why Christians in the Present Day Possess less Joy Than the Primitive Disciples

Dear brethren,

While the judgments of God are abroad in the earth, and multitudes are trembling for the fate of nations, and dreading lest famine, or war, or pestilence, which have desolated other countries, should receive a commission to lay waste our own, we have reason to bless God that he has manifested his care of his churches, by continuing the gospel among us, and granting it to be attended with some increasing success. The wall of Jerusalem is built up even in troublous times; and we were not only permitted to assemble in peace, but received tidings from most of the churches of a peculiarly pleasing nature.

In our letter of last year we addressed you on the nature and grounds of joy in God. In pursuance of the resolution of the last

---

[1] From *The Complete Works of the Rev. Andrew Fuller*, ed. Joseph Belcher (1845, Harrisonburg, VA: Sprinkle Publications, 1988), III, 325–331.

association, we shall in this attempt an answer to the following inquiry: why is it that Christians in the present day come so far short of the primitive Christians in the possession of joy?

That the thing itself is a fact can admit but little doubt. It is true, the joy of the primitive Christians was not always the same: previous to the resurrection and ascension of Christ they appeared to possess it in a far less degree than afterwards; and in their brightest days they, no doubt, as well as we, occasionally experienced intervening clouds. The account, nevertheless, which is given of them, intimates that a vein of sacred enjoyment ran through their lives. No sooner had they beheld the Lord Jesus taken up into heaven than they returned "to Jerusalem with great joy, and were continually in the temple, praising and blessing God."[2] And after the day of Pentecost, and the addition of three thousand souls by the preaching of Peter, they are described as: "continuing daily with one accord in the temple, and eating their meat with gladness and singleness of heart."[3] Persecution itself did not destroy their happiness, but helped, on some considerations, to increase it. Having been summoned before the Jewish council for preaching Christ, they "departed, rejoicing that they were counted worthy to suffer shame for his name's sake."[4] Covered with stripes, thrust into an inner prison, and with their feet made fast in the stocks, "at midnight Paul and Silas prayed, and sung praises to God!"[5] Nor was this happy frame of mind confined to the apostles, or to the first few years after the introduction of Christianity: Peter could say of the generality of Christians at the time when he wrote his first epistle, "Whom having not seen, ye love; in whom, though now ye see him not, yet, believing, ye rejoice with joy unspeakable, and full of glory."[6]

---

[2] Luke 24:53.
[3] Acts 2:46.
[4] Acts 5:41.
[5] Acts 16:25.
[6] 1 Peter 1:8.

Less Joy Than the Primitive Disciples

Such accounts of the primitive disciples afford an affecting view of the great disparity between them and the generality of modern Christians. The following particulars, amongst others, must needs strike an attentive observer.

First, they rejoiced in all their labours, complying with the commands of Christ rather as an honour and a privilege than as mere matter of duty. The prompt and cheerful manner in which they attended to divine institutions exhibits a lovely picture of genuine Christianity: "They that gladly received the word were baptized. And they continued steadfastly in the apostles' doctrine and fellowship, and in breaking of bread, and in prayers."[7] There is not a single instance in all the New Testament of an avowed Christian living in the neglect of the ordinances of Christ. Such an idea seems never to have entered into their minds; but it is unnecessary to say that with us it is a common case.

Secondly, they rejoiced, as we have seen, in tribulation, considering the reproaches of the world as an honour, and counting it all joy when they fell into divers temptations: but the highest exercises of grace that are common amongst us fall short in this particular; instead of rejoicing in tribulation, we are ready to account it pretty much if we rejoice notwithstanding it.

Thirdly, they experienced an habitual consciousness of their being the subjects of gracious dispositions, and consequently enjoyed a settled persuasion of their interest in Christ. In all the New Testament we have scarcely an instance of a Christian being at a loss to perceive the evidence of his Christianity. What are called doubts and fears amongst us, and which make up so large a proportion of our religious experiences, seem to have occupied scarcely any place amongst them. This fact, if there were no other, calls for serious inquiry into the cause or causes of it. The language that we are in the habit of using, when speaking of our love, or faith, or obedience,

---

[7] Acts 2:42.

betrays a sad defect in the exercise of these heavenly graces. Instead of being able to say, "O Lord, thou knowest all things, thou knowest that I love thee"[8]—"I have believed, and therefore have I spoken"[9]— "God, whom I serve in the gospel,"[10] and the like, we are ready to be startled at such professions, and feel ourselves under a kind of necessity to soften the language into a wish, a willingness, or a desire. "I desire to love, I would believe, I wish to be obedient," are expressions which frequently occur in our prayers and hymns; but wishing to love, and desiring to obey, when substituted in the place of love and obedience themselves, are inadmissible. Such language is unknown in the Scriptures, unless it be found in the character of the slothful, whose desire is said to kill him; and indicates, to say the least, but a small degree of real religion.

To account for this disparity is of importance, as by a knowledge of the causes of a malady we may be directed to the proper means of a cure. Peculiar dejection in individuals may often be accounted for from the peculiarity of their habits, constitution, circumstances, opportunities, and connexions; but when it affects a body or generation of men, it must be traced to other causes. Why should not we go on our way rejoicing in the same manner, and to the same degree, as the primitive Christians? We have the same gospel, the same promises, and the same hopes. The joy and peace which they experienced was in believing: the great, interesting, and transporting truths of the gospel were the source whence they derived their bliss. The Lord Messiah was come according to promise, and by laying down his life had delivered all who should believe in him from the wrath to come. Through his death also they were freed from the spirit of bondage attendant on the former dispensation, and received the Spirit of adoption, whereby they cried, "Abba, Father."[11] The thunders of

---

[8] John 21:17.
[9] Psalm 116:10; 2 Corinthians 4:13.
[10] Romans 1:9.
[11] Romans 8:15.

Less Joy Than the Primitive Disciples

Sinai gave place to the blessings of Zion, the city of the living God; to the holy society of which, as to a kind of heaven upon earth, they were introduced. Commissioned to publish these glad tidings to every creature, and persuaded that the cause in which they had engaged would sooner or later universally prevail, they laboured with courage and unwearied assiduity, and the work of the Lord prospered in their hands. Finally, in hope of eternal life, the joy set before them, like their Lord and Master, they endured the cross, despised the shame, and went and sat down with him on his throne, as he had overcome, and sat down with his Father on his throne.

Now which of these sources of joy has been exhausted? Are not Christ and the gospel, and its promises, the same yesterday, today, and forever? Is not God as willing now that the heirs of promise should have strong consolation as he was formerly? Are not the great blessings of eternal life as real and as interesting in the present age as in any that have gone before? And being promised to the smallest degree of real grace, even to the giving of a cup of cold water to a disciple of Jesus because he belongs to him, can it, in ordinary cases, be a difficult matter for a decided friend of Christ to obtain a clear satisfaction of his interest in them? Wherefore is it then, if the Son hath made us free, that we are not, in the most extensive meaning of the term, free indeed?

Some would probably attribute the whole to divine sovereignty, alleging that the Holy Spirit divideth to every age and generation, as well as to every man, severally as he will. It is allowed that the Holy Spirit, in all his gifts and operations, acts in a way of sovereignty, since we have no claim upon him for anything which he bestows; but it does not belong to the idea of sovereignty that there be no reason for it, or wisdom in it. The Holy Spirit divideth to every age and every man severally as he will, but he always willeth what is wise and good, or what is best upon the whole. The sovereignty of creatures may degenerate into caprice; but this cannot be supposed of God.

Now it belongs to the wisdom of God to bestow his favours in such a way as to encourage righteousness, and stamp an honour upon the means of his own appointment; hence it is that the joys of salvation, though bestowed in a way of sovereignty, are generally connected with a close walk with God, and communicated through means adapted to the end.

It has been thought by others that the difference betwixt us and the primitive Christians, in these things, may be accounted for, at least in some degree, by a difference of circumstances. Life and immortality were brought to light, as the Scriptures express it, by the gospel. The wonderful transition therefore which they experienced, some of them from the darkness of Judaism, and others from the still grosser darkness of paganism, together with the great success of their labours, must have forcibly impressed their minds with both surprise and joy. There is some truth, no doubt, in this observation; but it ought to be considered, on the other hand, that our circumstances are in some respects more favourable to joy than theirs; sufficiently so perhaps to balance, if not overbalance, those in which theirs were superior to ours. Let the following things be considered in connexion with each other:

First, glorious things are spoken in prophecy of what shall be done for the church in the last periods of time. All the light and glory that have ever yet appeared will be eclipsed by what is to come. One peculiar characteristic of the kingdom of Christ is that it is progressive. God is saying to his church under every new dispensation, or period of her existence, "Remember not the former things, neither consider the things of old: behold, I do a new thing in the earth."[12] As if he should say, you may forget the past, and yet have enough to fill you with joyful admiration. The Jewish dispensation contained a greater display of God than had ever been made before; yet, compared with the dawn of gospel glory, it was but as the moon to the

---

[12] Isaiah 43:18–19.

LESS JOY THAN THE PRIMITIVE DISCIPLES

sun; and glorious as this was, with regard to all that had gone before, it will bear no comparison to that which is to follow after. Not only shall "the moon be confounded," but "the sun ashamed, when the Lord of hosts shall reign in Mount Zion, and before his ancients gloriously!"[13]

Secondly, the time when things shall be accomplished cannot be very far off. The sacred writers of the New Testament frequently intimate that they had passed the meridian of time, and were entered, as it were, into the afternoon of the world. They speak of their times as the last days, and of themselves as those "on whom the ends of the world were come." They declared that, "the end of all things was at hand;"[14] that the Judge was "at the door;"[15] and the concluding warning of the book of God is couched in this strong expression, "Surely, I come quickly!"[16] But if the end of all things was then at hand, what must we think of it after a lapse of nearly 1800 years?

Thirdly, it is highly probable, if not more than probable, that in the ages yet to come there may be much more effected than in all preceding ages put together. Some of the greatest events in prophecy we know remain to be accomplished; particularly, the utter downfall of Antichrist, the conversion of the Jews, and the universal spread of true religion but if the end of all things be at hand, and such great events are first to be accomplished, we have every reason to expect great changes, in quick succession, and at no great distance of time. The convulsions of the present day may, for aught we know, be some of the throes of creation travailing in pain for the glorious liberty of the sons of God. At all events, the day of the church's redemption draweth nigh; it is time therefore to "lift up our heads,"[17] and to go forth in prayer, and praise, and joyful exertion to meet the

---

[13] Isaiah 24:23.
[14] 1 Peter 4:7.
[15] James 5:9.
[16] Revelation 22:20.
[17] Psalm 24:7.

Bridegroom. Could the apostles and primitive Christians have been placed in our situation, they would have rejoiced with joy unspeakable and full of glory. We must turn our attention then to some other objects besides the circumstances in which we are placed as the causes of our want of joy.

We pass over the cases of such as indulge themselves in known sin, or live in the neglect of known duty, as cases easily accounted for, at one period of time as well as another; and confine our inquiry to those whose conversation is allowed in general to be regular and circumspect; so much so, at least, as to be equal to that of the body of professing Christians around them.

In the first place, let it be considered whether it does not arise from the want of a greater degree of religion in general. Joy is a grace which cannot thrive by itself; it is a kind of appendage to the lively exercise of other graces:

- "With joy shall ye draw water out of the wells of salvation."[18]
- "Hitherto ye have asked nothing in my name; ask, and receive, that your joy may be full."[19]
- "The kingdom of God is righteousness, peace, and joy in the Holy Ghost."[20]

From these passages, and many others which might be cited, it is apparent that holy joy stands connected with appropriating the great truths of the gospel to our particular cases—with importunate prayer in the name of Christ—and with the practice of righteousness and peace. The same persons who were daily employed in praising and blessing God have this testimony given of them, "and great grace was upon them all."

---

[18] Isaiah 12:3.
[19] John 16:24.
[20] Romans 14:17.

Less Joy Than the Primitive Disciples

Secondly, let it be considered whether another reason be not our neglect of a more frequent and intense application to those objects whence joy arises. We have seen already, that the sources from which the primitive Christians derived their joy were the great doctrines of the gospel; but it is a lamentable fact, that the generality of professing Christians amongst us content themselves with a very superficial knowledge of these things. There are but few even amongst the godly in our day, that so enter into the spirit and glory of the gospel as clearly to distinguish it from error speciously disguised. Hence, if a minister who is much respected by his people turn aside from even important truth, it is common for many of them to go off with him.

If Christians were properly rooted and grounded in the gospel—if they understood not only what they believe, but wherefore they believe it—they would not be shaken with every wind of doctrine; nor would many of the principles which prevail in the present age excite even a momentary hesitation in their minds. But if we do not so understand the truth as clearly to distinguish it from error, it cannot be supposed that we should be greatly affected by it. It is by drawing waters from the wells of salvation that we have joy; but these wells are deep, and, in proportion as we are wanting in an understanding of divine things, we may be said to have nothing to draw with.

Thirdly, to this may be added the want of public spirit. The primitive Christians were all intent on disseminating the gospel through the world; and it was in the midst of this kind of employment, and the persecutions which attended it, that they are said to have been "filled with joy and the Holy Ghost."[21] Much of the joyful part of religion is lost by rendering it the immediate object of our pursuit. The chief end for which great numbers read their Bibles, and hear the word, is that they may be comforted, and obtain some

---

[21] Acts 13:52.

satisfaction of their being in a state of salvation; but this is not the way in which the comforts of the gospel are obtained. There are things which, if pursued as our chief end, will elude our grasp and vanish from our sight: such is reputation amongst men, and such is religious joy. If we pursue the public good, not for the sake of applause, but from a disinterested regard to the well-being of our species, reputation will follow us; and if the glory of God and the prosperity of his cause occupy the first place in our affection, we shall not in ordinary cases be wanting in peace and heavenly consolation. If a portion of that time which we spend in ransacking for evidence in the mass of past experiences, were employed in promoting the cause of God in the world, and seeking the welfare of the souls and bodies of men, it would turn to a better account. In seeking the salvation of others we should find our own. The love of Zion has the promise of personal prosperity. Ardently to promote the honour of God, and the good of mankind, is itself an evidence, and the highest evidence, of true religion: while, therefore, we feel conscious of the purity of our present motives, we have less occasion for reflections on the past.

There is a much greater satisfaction too in this way of obtaining comfort than in the other; for however former exercises of grace might be strong and decisive at the time, yet it must be difficult to realize them merely by a distant recollection. It is much better also, and more for our profit, to live in the exercise of grace, than barely to remember that we did so at some former period of our lives. We appeal to your own hearts, brethren, with respect to your late disinterested exertions for carrying the gospel amongst the heathen, we appeal to those of you especially who have had the undertaking most at heart, whether, since your own comfort has in a sort been overlooked, and swallowed up in concern for the salvation of others, you have not felt more of the joyful part of religion than you did before; yea, may we not add, more than at any former period in your remembrance?

Fourthly, much may be owing to our viewing the mixture of evils which pervade creation on a contracted scale. If the evils which befall creatures be considered merely as evils, and our minds are disposed to pore upon them, we must necessarily feel dejected; but if every partial evil contribute to the general good—if every adversity, whether it respect our persons, families, Christian connexions, country, or species, be but as a wheel acting upon other wheels, and all necessary to complete the vast but well-ordered machinery—the contemplation of evil itself in this view must raise the heart instead of depressing it. The miseries of the present and of the future life, if contemplated by a good man merely as evils, must overwhelm him and destroy his present peace. What can he do? He cannot shun the abodes of the wretched in this world, and so put the thoughts of their miseries far from him, for that were inhumanity; neither can he allow himself to doubt of the execution of, divine threatenings in the world to come, for that were to arraign the justice, goodness, wisdom, and veracity of God in denouncing them: but he may view things on an enlarged scale, and thus perceive that all is right and best upon the whole. This is to be of one mind with God, and so to be truly happy. It is in this way that we are reconciled to our own adversities: could Jacob have seen through the gracious designs of God with regard to his children, or, though he might be unable to do this, had he properly recollected the divine promise, "I will surely do thee good,"[22] he would not have concluded, as he did, that all these things were against him.

It is thus that upon some occasions we are reconciled to the miseries of a public execution. Awful beyond conception it must be to the party who suffer; but justice may require the sacrifice. However natural affection, therefore, may for a moment revolt at the idea of inflicting death, all concern for a suffering individual is absorbed by the love of our species, and a regard for the general good. It is thus

---

[22] Genesis 32:12.

that the heavenly inhabitants are described as being not only reconciled to the overthrow of mystical Babylon, but as rejoicing in it. While the merchants who traded in her wares bitterly lament her fall, crying, "Alas! alas! that great city! In one hour is she made desolate!"[23] the friends of God are called to a very different employment:

> Rejoice over her, thou heaven, and ye holy apostles and prophets, for God hath avenged you on her. ... And after these things I heard a great voice of much people in heaven saying, Hallelujah! True and righteous are his judgments, for he hath judged the great whore, which did corrupt the earth with her fornication, and hath avenged the blood of his servants at her hand. And again they said, Hallelujah and her smoke rose up for ever and ever![24]

Was there any malevolence or unchristian bitterness in all this? No: it was only viewing things on a large scale; viewing them as God views them, and feeling accordingly.

The primitive Christians were in the habit of considering all things as working together for good, and so of deriving joy from every occurrence. If the world smiled upon them, they rejoiced, and availed themselves of the opportunity for spreading the gospel; or if it frowned on them for their attachment to Christ, they rejoiced that they were counted worthy to suffer shame for his name's sake. By thus converting every thing into food for joy, they answered to the exhortations of the apostles, "Let the brother of low degree rejoice that he is exalted; but the rich in that he is made low."[25]—"Beloved, count it all joy when ye fall into divers temptations."[26]—"Rejoice evermore. ... In every thing give thanks."[27] If we would feel like

---

[23] Revelation 18:19.
[24] Revelation 18:20; 19:1-3.
[25] James 1:9.
[26] James 1:2.
[27] 1 Thessalonians 5:16, 18.

them, we must enter into their views; we must have less of the complaining patriarch, as well as of the whining merchants; and more of that temper which prompted the holy inhabitants of heaven, on every new dispensation of providence, to cry, "Amen, Hallelujah!"

Fifthly, much is owing, no doubt, to a spirit of conformity to the present world, by which many Christians, especially those in prosperous circumstances, are influenced. It was a complaint made by one of the fathers, Cyprian, in the middle of the third century, a time when the church had enjoyed a considerable respite from persecution, that "each one studied how to increase his patrimony, and, forgetting what the faithful had done in apostolic times, or what they ought always to do, their great passion was an insatiable desire of enlarging their fortunes."[28]

This complaint, everyone knows, is too applicable to our times. The primitive Christians were persecuted. The Waldenses,[29] the Reformers, the Puritans, and the Nonconformists were the same; and, having but little security for property, they had but little motive to increase it being driven also from the society of their persecutors, they were under very little temptation to imitate their manners; their trials were great, but they were of a different kind from ours. Having long enjoyed the blessings of religious liberty, we have relaxed in watchfulness, and the world has seemed in a measure to have lost its enmity, and to smile upon us. In consequence of this we have become upon more friendly terms with it; not merely by behaving courteously and affectionately to men in common, which is our duty; but

---

[28] Cyprian, *On the Lapsed* 6. Cyprian of Carthage (*c.*200-258) was a key bishop in the Latin-speaking North African Church of the third century. For help in identifying this quote, I am indebted to D. Forrest Mills, who is writing his doctoral dissertation on Cyprian at The Southern Baptist Theological Seminary.

[29] The Waldensians, founded by Pierre Vaudès (*c.*1140–*c.*1205), sought to reform the medieval church in the twelfth century. On the Waldensian movement, see Euan Cameron, *Waldenses: Rejection of Holy Church in Medieval Europe* (Oxford: Blackwell, 2000) and Peter Biller, *The Waldensians, 1170-1530: Between a Religious Order and a Church* (New York, NY: Routledge, 2001).

by imbibing their spirit, courting their company, and subjecting ourselves to a servile compliance with their customs.

These things were extremely unfriendly to true religion. If the cares of this world be compared to thorns, which choke the Word, the alluring pleasures of it are with no less propriety compared to the burning sun, through whose influence many a promising plant has withered away. Or, should the root of the matter be found in us, yet if our heads and hearts are occupied with appearance, dress, entertainments, and the like, there can be but little room for heaven or heavenly things; and consequently this joyful part of religion will be slighted and lost.

Finally, it is not to be dissembled that much is to be traced to the manner in which the gospel is preached. The Holy Spirit ordinarily works by means of the Word. It is the office of ministers to be "helpers of your joy;" but if they partake of the spirit common to the age in which they live, their preaching will partake of it too. If the great and interesting truths of the gospel are not thoroughly understood, and felt, they cannot, in the ordinary course of things, be communicated in such a manner as greatly to interest the hearts of others. While, therefore, we recommend serious reflection to you, brethren, you also have a right to expect the same of us; and we trust we are willing to receive as well as to administer the Word of exhortation. Dear brethren, farewell!

Questions

1. How does Fuller envisage God exercising his judgments in history? Is his thinking biblical? Indicate how.
2. According to Fuller, why did "a vein of sacred enjoyment" run through the lives of the first Christians?
3. What have been the various reasons suggested for the difference between the joy of the first Christians and the emotive state of those of Fuller's day?
4. What do you learn about Fuller's eschatology from these pages?
5. What was the ground of the joy of the early Christians?
6. What is the danger of making the pursuit of "religious joy" as one's "chief end"?
7. As the fourth reason for the difference between the first Christians and those of his day, Fuller says it is owing to "the miseries of the present and of the future life, [which] if contemplated by a good man merely as evils, must overwhelm him and destroy his present peace." What does Fuller recommend as a solution to this problem?
8. How does Fuller view capital punishment?
9. Why are "the blessings of religious liberty" a factor in the loss of Christian joy?
10. What do you learn about Fuller's thoughts about church history from these sentences, "The primitive Christians were persecuted. The Waldenses, the Reformers, the Puritans, and the Nonconformists were the same"?
11. What is the final reason that Fuller believes accounts for the difference in the level of joy? What does this final reason reveal about Fuller's view of preaching?

Jesus being baptized by John
(the frontispiece of Robert Robinson,
The History of Baptism [1790])

7
The Practical Uses of Christian Baptism[1]
(1802)

Introduction

It is curious that Baptists have spent far more energy defining the mode of baptism and delineating its proper subjects than they have in determining the meaning of baptism. In this text, which also began as a circular letter for the Northamptonshire Association, Andrew Fuller set forth one of the clearest and richest discussions of the meaning of baptism in the Baptist tradition.

The Practical Uses of Christian Baptism

Dear brethren,

In connexion with our last general letter, and agreeably to the appointment made at the yearly meeting, we now address you on a subject, not only of general interest, but which more immediately relates to that solemn profession which you have made of Christianity; namely, the practical uses of the ordinance of baptism.

That Christian baptism is properly administered only by immersion, and to those who make a credible profession of faith in Christ, it is no part of our present design to prove. Addressing you, we shall take each of these particulars for granted. The only subject to which we now request your attention is the influence of this ordinance, where it produces its proper effects, in promoting piety in individuals, and purity in the church.

---

[1] From *The Complete Works of the Rev. Andrew Fuller*, ed. Joseph Belcher (1845, Harrisonburg, VA: Sprinkle Publications, 1988), III, 339–345.

There is no part of true religion that is merely speculative; the whole is designed and adapted to sanctify the soul. We may presume, therefore, that if baptism be an ordinance of God, and of perpetual obligation in the church, it is of importance to Christian practice.

But it is not on presumptive evidence that we wish to rest the improvement of this institution, any more than the institution itself; neither shall we go about to connect with it acknowledged duties by imaginary alliances; but shall confine ourselves to those uses of the ordinance which are actually made, or suggested, in the New Testament. We could address many things to parents, and things of importance too, on bringing up their children in the nurture and admonition of the Lord: we could also urge it upon the children of believers that they were committed to God from their earliest infancy; but as we find nothing of this kind in the Scriptures connected with baptism, however important these things would be in their place, they would be altogether irrelevant while treating on this ordinance.

Baptism is a divine institution, pertaining to the kingdom of the Messiah, or the gospel dispensation. John received it from heaven, and administered it to the Jews, who, on his proclaiming that the kingdom of heaven was at hand, confessed their sins. Jesus gave sanction to it by his example; and after his resurrection, when all power in heaven and earth was committed to him, he confirmed and extended it to believers of all nations. Whatever circumstantial differences there might be, therefore, between the baptism of John and that of Christ, they were substantially the same. There were things in former ages which bore a resemblance to it; as the salvation of Noah and his family in the ark, the passage of the Israelites through the sea, divers washings or bathings prescribed by the Mosaic ritual, etc.; but the thing itself existed not, till it was revealed to the immediate forerunner of Christ.

The principal design of it appears to be a solemn and practical profession of the Christian religion. Such was the baptism of John,

Uses of Christian Baptism

who "said unto the people, that they should believe on him who should come after him; that is, on Christ Jesus."[2] And such was that in the times of the apostles. Paul addressing himself to the churches in Galatia, who, after having professed to believe in Christ, cleaved to the Mosaic law as a medium of justification, thus speaks:

> The law was our schoolmaster to bring us to Christ, that we might be justified by faith; but after that faith is come, we are no longer under a schoolmaster. For ye are all the children of God by faith in Christ Jesus. For as many of you as have been baptized into Christ have put on Christ.[3]

The allusion is to the putting on of apparel, as when one that enters into the service of a prince puts on his distinguishing attire; and the design of the sacred writer is to remind those of them who had before professed the Jewish religion, that by a solemn act of their own they had, as it were, put off Moses, and put on Christ. There is a putting on of Christ which is internal, and consists in relinquishing the former lusts, and being of the mind of Christ; but that which is here referred to appears to be an open profession of his name, to the renouncing of every thing that stood in competition with him. It was therefore true of as many as had been baptized, whether they abode in the truth or not. And even their being "the children of God by faith in Christ Jesus"[4] seems to express what they were in profession, rather than what they were in fact. They had by their baptism disowned all dependence on the privileges of birth, and the adoption which pertained to them as the children of Abraham; and declared their acquiescence in that power, or privilege, to become the sons of God, which the gospel imparts to them that believe. The mention of this was perfectly in point, as it greatly heightened the evil of their

---

[2] Acts 19:4.
[3] Galatians 3:24–27.
[4] Galatians 3:26.

defection. The amount is that as many as were baptized in the primitive ages were voluntary agents, and submitted to this ordinance for the purpose of making a solemn and practical profession of the Christian faith. It was their oath of allegiance to the King of Zion; that by which they avowed the Lord to be their God. Hence a rejection of it involved a rejection of the counsel of God. The sin of the Pharisees and lawyers consisted, not in their refusing to submit to baptism as unbelievers; but in not embracing the Messiah, and so putting on the badge of his profession. Their rejection of the sign was justly construed as a rejection of the thing signified; as when a rebel refuses to take the oath of allegiance, it is construed as a refusal of submission and subjection to his rightful prince.

Such, brethren, is the profession we have made. We have not only declared in words our repentance towards God, and faith towards our Lord Jesus Christ; but have said the same things by our baptism. We have solemnly surrendered ourselves up to Christ, taking him to be our Prophet, Priest, and King; engaging to receive his doctrine, to rely on his atonement, and to obey his laws. The vows of God are upon us. We have even sworn to keep his righteous judgments; and, without violating the oath of God, we cannot go back. If it be a sin not to confess the Lord Jesus, through fear or shame, it is a still greater sin, after we have confessed him, to turn from the holy commandment.

The religion of Jesus consists partly of truths to be believed, and partly of precepts to be obeyed; and the ordinance of baptism furnishes motives for a faithful adherence to both.

We have been baptized "in the name of the Father, and of the Son, and of the Holy Spirit;"[5] and have thus practically avowed our belief in them. It was at Jordan that the Father bore witness to his well-beloved Son, and that the Holy Spirit descended upon him; hither, therefore, in the early ages, men were directed to repair, that

---

[5] Matthew 28:19.

they might learn the doctrine of the Trinity. If we relinquish this doctrine, we virtually relinquish our baptism. Of this there need not be a more convincing proof, than the inclination which has been discovered by those who have renounced the doctrine to disuse the form of baptizing in the name of the Sacred Three.

We have also professed by our baptism to embrace that great salvation which is accomplished by the united influence of the Sacred Three. We have in effect declared our acquiescence in the freeness of the Father's grace, in the all-sufficient atonement of the Son, and in the sanctifying influence of the Holy Spirit; for these are the principal things by which, in the New Testament account of the economy of grace, each is distinguished. Nor can we renounce them, without virtually renouncing our baptism.

The immersion of the body in water, which is a purifying element, contains a profession of our faith in Christ, through the shedding of whose blood we are cleansed from all sin. Hence, baptism in the name of Christ is said to be for the remission of sins. Not that there is any such virtue in the element, whatever be the quantity; nor in the ceremony, though of divine appointment: but it contains a sign of the way in which we must be saved. Sin is washed away in baptism in the same sense as Christ's flesh is eaten, and his blood drank, in the Lord's supper: the sign, when rightly used, leads to the thing signified. Remission of sins is ascribed by Peter not properly to baptism, but to the name in which the parties were to be baptized. Thus also Saul was directed to wash away his sins, calling on the name of the Lord.[6] Nearly akin to this is the idea conveyed to us in the first epistle of Peter:

> The long-suffering of God waited in the days of Noah, while the ark was preparing, wherein few, that is, eight souls, were saved by water. The like figure whereunto baptism doth now

[6] Acts 22:16.

save us (not the putting away of the filth of the flesh, but the answer of a good conscience towards God) by the resurrection of Jesus Christ.[7]

The salvation of Noah and his family by the ark was a figure of our salvation by the death and resurrection of Jesus Christ. The ark for a time was surrounded, as it were, with waters from above, and from beneath; but it survived its trial, and those who were in it were at length brought safe to land. Christ, also, for a time sustained the deluge of wrath due to our sins; but survived the trial, rising triumphantly from the dead, and thereby saved us from everlasting death. Of this great transaction baptism is a like figure. It is another sign of the same thing. The resemblance of baptism by immersion to the death and resurrection of Christ, and the suitableness of the one to signify our faith in the other, are manifest. It is thus that baptism does now save us; not as putting away the filth of the flesh (for all the virtue contained in the ordinance itself is "the answer of a good conscience toward God"), but as affording a sign of our salvation by the victorious resurrection of our Lord Jesus Christ.

And as we are taught by our baptism to adhere to the doctrine of God our Saviour, so we are furnished with motives to adorn it by a holy conversation. Thus it is introduced in the Epistles to the Romans and Colossians, as a sign of our being dead and buried to the principles and pursuits of the present world; and, by faith in Christ, raised as into a new world. The death of Christ is emphatically mentioned as that into which we are baptized:

> Know ye not that so many of us as were baptized into Jesus Christ were baptized into his death? Therefore we are buried with him by baptism into death; that like as Christ died, and

---

[7] 1 Peter 3:20–21.

was raised up from the dead by the glory of the Father, even so we also should walk in newness of life.[8]

Christ's dying for sin afforded a most powerful motive for our dying to it; and the immersion of the body in baptism, being in the likeness of the former, furnishes an additional motive to the latter.

The leading idea suggested by a death and burial seems to be that of separation from the world. There is no greater line of separation than that which is drawn between the dead and the living. "The dead know not any thing; and have no portion in all that is done under the sun."[9] Such is the line which is drawn by the faith of the operation of God between the world renewed and the world depraved, of which baptism is the appointed sign. If, after this, we are found among evildoers, we may well be considered and shunned as a kind of apparitions, which have no proper concern in the affairs of mortals.

The apostle applied this reasoning against a conformity to abrogated ceremonies: "If ye be dead with Christ from the rudiments of the world, why, as though living in the world, are ye subject to ordinances?"[10] The same reasoning is applicable to other things: If we be dead with Christ, why, as though living, are we subject to the lust of the flesh, the lust of the eye, and the pride of life, which are of the world? Why are any of us conformed to this world; and not rather transformed by the renewing of our minds? If we be dead, and our life be hid with Christ in God, why are not our affections set on things above, and not on things on the earth? We cannot but express our concern that persons professing godliness should be carried away by the course of this world, as many are; meanly imitating the ungodly, whose conduct they ought rather to reprove. Such imitation, so far as it operates, contains a virtual renunciation of our baptism. The ideas of baptism and a separation from the world, whether

---

[8] Romans 6:3-4.
[9] Ecclesiastes 9:5.
[10] Colossians 2:20.

connected by us or not, are strongly associated in the minds of men in general. After this, we cannot unite with them in evil, without drawing upon ourselves their most pointed censures. They may labour to seduce us for the sake of comforting themselves; and while accomplishing their purpose may suppress their private thoughts of us, and even compliment us for our liberality; but if we comply, their pretended esteem will be turned into reproach. Nor ought we to consider this as an evil; but rather as a mercy. God has hereby set a hedge about us, which tends more than a little to preserve us from temptation. If any think otherwise, and feel uneasy that they cannot act like other men, without drawing upon themselves the censures of mankind, it is a dark sign that their hearts are not right in the sight of God.

Nor is this ordinance adapted merely to separate between believers and unbelievers individually considered; its design is also to draw a line of distinction between the kingdom of Christ and the kingdom of Satan. Whatever may be said of baptism as it is now generally understood and practised, and of the personal religion of those who practise it, it was originally appointed to be the boundary of visible Christianity. This is a principle which, if properly acted upon, would go far to prevent the confounding of the church and the world; and which, consequently, tends more than any thing of the kind to counteract ecclesiastical degeneracy and corruption. Had the Christian church in all ages admitted none to baptism, from whomsoever descended, but those who professed to repent and believe the gospel, it is scarcely conceivable that any others would have been admitted to the Lord's supper; and if so, a stream of corruption which has actually deluged it with anti-Christianism would have been diverted at the springhead.

The church might, indeed, have been corrupted from other causes, but these would have been merely accidental. Hypocrites and formalists might have imposed themselves upon it, as they did

USES OF CHRISTIAN BAPTISM

in some degree in the apostolic age; but they would have been intruders. Whatever of this kind might have existed, believers could not have been constitutionally yoked together with unbelievers. The carnal descendants of godly people could not have claimed a place in Christ's visible kingdom. The church could not have become national, embracing as its children all who are born in a Christianized country, without any profession of personal religion. Princes and nobles, if worthy, would have been received into its communion as brethren; but not as rulers or patrons: and, if unworthy, refused; even though an exposure to persecution had been the consequence. But if persons be admitted to baptism without any profession of personal religion, or upon the profession of others on their behalf, their admission to the Lord's supper will in most cases follow as a matter of course. Indeed it ought to follow; for though among evangelical Dissenters these things are separated, yet from the beginning it was not so. Neither Scripture nor the practice of the ancient churches affords a single example of a baptized person, unless his conduct was grossly immoral, being ineligible to communion. And if all who are now baptized be admitted to the supper, the line of separation will be broken; the church will be no longer a garden enclosed, but an open wilderness, where every beast of prey can range at pleasure. Thus, indeed, it was foretold it should be. The writer of the Apocalypse, describing the corruptions which should prevail in the visible church during the twelve hundred and sixty years' reign of antichrist, represents it under the form of the outer court of the temple being left out of the measurement as profane, and given to the Gentiles to be trodden under foot, in like manner as the holy place and holy city had been trodden down by the heathen, in the time of Antiochus.

As the principle of believers' baptism, properly acted upon, would prevent the admission of all unconverted characters, except hypocrites and self-deceivers, so it would have its influence in repelling them. The habits of some hypocritical characters, it is true, would render it an easy thing to overleap this boundary; but it is equally true that to others it would be an effectual bar. There are not a few in the religious world who would like well to be members of a Christian church, especially where the pastor is a man of respectability, provided they could be admitted without drawing upon themselves the laugh of the irreligious. There is reason to believe that many persons of genteel connexions, who wish to be thought religious, and whose consciences approve of believers' baptism, are withheld by this kind of shame from offering themselves to our churches. An ordinance which thus operates possesses a mark of its pertaining to that kingdom which is not of this world, and into which it is hard for a rich man to enter.

As the leading idea suggested by a death and burial is that of separation from the world, so the principal thing denoted by a resurrection is an entrance into a new state of being. Such is that newness of life of which the emersion of the body from the waters of baptism is a sign, and to which it furnishes an important motive. The religion of Jesus does not consist in mere negatives. It is not enough that we be dead to the world; we must be alive to God. With real Christians old things are passed away, and all things are become new. Unless our baptism, therefore, be merely a sign, or an unmeaning ceremony, our hopes, fears, sorrows, joys, companions, principles, and pursuits are opposite to those of this world. Even a partial return to it is inconsistent with our baptismal vows. If those who profess to be dead to the world cannot walk in the course of it without being considered and shunned as a kind of apparitions, those who are alive from the dead cannot return without resembling a living character who should take up his abode in a sepulchre.

A few general reflections will conclude this epistle. The baptism of a number of serious Christians is an interesting and impressive spectacle! Often on such solemn occasions have we witnessed the falling tear; not only from the parties baptized, and others immediately connected with them, but from indifferent spectators. We could appeal to the consciences of many serious Christians, whether they did not receive their first convictions of the reality of religion at such opportunities. We could appeal to all of you, who have been in the habit of attending the administration of this ordinance, whether it has not frequently furnished you with the most solemn and tender reflections. Has not the sight of a number of young Christians, offering themselves willingly to the Lord, touched the secret springs of holy sensibility? Yes; you have been reminded by it of your own solemn engagements, and led to inquire in what manner they have been fulfilled. You have remembered the days of your espousals, when you first went after your Saviour as in the wilderness, and have been sweetly impelled to renew the solemn surrender. Nor have your reflections been confined to yourselves; you have considered these new accessions to the church of God as supplying the place of others that were taken away, and as fulfilling the promise, "Instead of thy fathers, shall be thy children."[11] When a number of dear friends and useful characters have, one after another, been removed by death, you have been ready to ask, "Who shall fill up their place; and by whom shall Jacob arise?" But when others of promising gifts and graces have come forward and yielded up themselves to the Lord in baptism, they have seemed in a manner to be "baptized for the dead."[12] Thus, when the ranks of an army in a besieged city are thinned by repeated engagements, and the hearts of survivors are ready to faint, a reinforcement arrives: a body of new companions throw themselves in to its relief, and inspire them with new vigour.

Further, if the foregoing remarks be just, the importance of believers' baptism must appear in a very different light from that in which some have represented it. If the ordinary acknowledgments of

---

[11] Psalm 45:16.
[12] 1 Corinthians 15:29.

many who live in the neglect of this ordinance, and disapprove of the zeal of others who submit to it, may be considered as expressive of their principles, their conduct is not owing to a solid conviction, arising from impartial inquiry accompanied with prayer, that it is unscriptural, or that they have already been baptized according to the institution of Christ; but to a notion that it is of little or no account. If it be of little or no account to bind ourselves to the Lord in the way of his own prescribing, to confess his name before men, to avow our being dead to the world, and alive to him, to preserve the church from being constitutionally corrupted, and yoked together with unbelievers, to obey his commandments who saith, "Repent, and be baptized every one of you;"[13] and to follow his example who yielded obedience to this institute, saying, "Thus it becometh us to fulfil all righteousness"[14] then may this excuse be admitted. But if these things be important, then is believers' baptism important; and all attempts to depreciate it are offensive in the sight of him who is the Lord and lawgiver of Zion.

Finally, brethren, it becomes us to beware lest that which is good in itself should, through the corruption of our nature, become an occasion of evil. There is, perhaps, no temptation more common among religious people than to think too highly of themselves on account of their advantages. Where such a spirit is cherished, baptism may become an idol, and the table of the Lord itself a snare. It is more than possible that some may so value themselves on account of their baptism, as to make it a substitute for a life of holiness and universal righteousness. It appears that some among the Corinthians approached too near, at least, to this spirit. They had been baptized ... they had eaten and drank at the table of the Lord ... yet they trifled with idolatry, and worldly lusts.

---

[13] Acts 2:38.
[14] Matthew 3:15.

USES OF CHRISTIAN BAPTISM

I would not that ye should be ignorant [said Paul], how that all our fathers were under the cloud, and all passed through the sea; and were all baptized unto Moses in the cloud, and in the sea; and did all eat the same spiritual meat; and did all drink the same spiritual drink (for they drank of that spiritual Rock that followed them, and that Rock was Christ). But with many of them God was not well pleased; for they were overthrown in the wilderness. Now these things were our examples ... Wherefore let him that thinketh he standeth take heed lest he fall![15]

As if he had said: Are you members of a community which has the promised presence of Christ? Our fathers also were "under the cloud." Has God interposed in your favour? They "passed through the sea," as on dry land. Have you been baptized? So were they. They "descended" in a body into the sea; were "buried," as it were, by the cloud above them and the waters on each hand of them; and afterwards "ascended" on the other side. Have you been admitted to the holy supper? They also ate of that food, and drank of that stream, the spiritual intent of which was much the same. Yet all this afforded them no security, when they provoked the divine jealousy. Notwithstanding these privileges they fell, and were destroyed of the destroyer. These things are recorded for our admonition. Of what account then will our baptism be to us, if, instead of being dead to the world and alive to God, we be the reverse? Will baptism save us? No: it will bear witness against us!

And though we may not fall into so fatal an error as to substitute baptism in the place of holiness, righteousness, and godliness; yet if we cherish a fond conceit of ourselves, magnifying our advantages to the neglect of a spirit of humble watchfulness, our baptism, instead of aiding us, will become a snare. We do not always act up to our advantages. It is very possible that Christians who are behind us in

---

[15] 1 Corinthians 10:1-6, 12

this particular, may notwithstanding be before us in their general character. It were vain and foolish to imagine that our possessing the truth in one instance will secure us from error in every other; or that our fulfilling this command of Christ, however important, will insure a course of universal obedience.

Let us never forget, that however adapted this or that ordinance, form, or mode of church government may be to promote our spiritual interests, yet if we rest in the means, they will deceive us; or rather we shall deceive ourselves. It is the presence of Christ only that can keep us alive, either as individuals or as churches. While, therefore, we recommend the means which he has prescribed, we devoutly add, with the apostle, "The grace of our Lord Jesus Christ, and the love of God, and the communion of the Holy Spirit, be with you all! Amen."[16]

---

[16] 2 Corinthians 13:14.

Questions

1. Why did God institute the ordinance of baptism?
2. What doctrines does baptism teach?
3. What is meant by the phrase that "the sign, when rightly used, leads to the thing signified"?
4. How does baptism inculcate a holy lifestyle?
5. What is the relationship in Fuller's mind between baptism and the church as a "garden enclosed"?
6. What role does baptism play according to Fuller's "general reflections"?
7. Why is believer's baptism not sufficient to maintain a life of genuine spirituality? What is necessary for such a life?

Samuel Hopkins

8
To the Christian Females of Great Britain[1]
(1802)

Introduction

The influence of Jonathan Edwards upon Andrew Fuller's thought has been noted in the "Introduction,"[2] but almost as influential was the thinking and works of some of Edwards' mentees, men like Samuel Hopkins (1721-1803) and Jonathan Edwards, Jr.,[3] whose thought became known as the "New Divinity." Fuller was judicious in his adaptation of the thinking of these theologians, but even so, there were critics like the London Particular Baptist Abraham Booth (1734-1806). Fuller had enormous admiration for Booth, who thought that these men's thinking on such matters as the atonement had led Fuller astray. Personally, I think Booth was wrong in this estimation, but his criticism stuck and in some quarters Fuller became known as the "American doctor"![4]

In 1802, Fuller with his closest living friends, John Ryland, Jr. and John Sutcliff (1752-1814), supervised the publication of a British edition of Samuel Hopkins' *Memoirs of Miss Susanna Anthony*, which first appeared in 1796. Susanna Anthony (1726-1791) had been born in Newport, Rhode Island, and lived a relatively uneventful life, though, as her diary reveals, she left a rich legacy of spirituality.

---

[1] From Samuel Hopkins, compiled, *Memoirs of Miss Susanna Anthony*, new ed. (Clipstone: J.W. Morris, 1802), i-viii.

[2] Also see Chris Chun, *The Legacy of Jonathan Edwards in the Theology of Andrew Fuller*, Studies in the History of Christian Traditions, vol. 162 (Leiden/Boston: Brill, 2012).

[3] See above pg. 74 in the text of Fuller's response to William Vidler.

[4] Edwards A. Park, *Memoir of the Life and Character of Samuel Hopkins, D.D.*, 2nd ed. (Boston, MA: Doctrinal Tract and Book Society, 1854), 223.

Hopkins brought together a number of extracts from her diary to create a picture of Evangelical piety that he hoped would influence both women and men. This presentation of a female model of piety is very Edwardsean as his mentor, Jonathan Edwards, also often recommended the spiritual experiences of women as exemplary.

To the Christian Females of Great Britain
Dear friends,

It is one of the glories of Christianity, that it knows neither Jew nor Greek, bond nor free, male nor female; but considers all as one in Christ Jesus.[5] As fellow-heirs of the same grace, we feel interested in your edification. While great numbers of your sex, who have leisure for reading, are wasting their time, and corrupting their minds with novels, and such kind of trash, we are persuaded you have a relish for better things.

In dedicating an English edition of the following *Memoirs* to you, we hope we shall be found to have presented you with what is both acceptable and useful. The lives of eminently holy persons furnish materials worthy of being recorded. A considerable part of the oracles of God consists in such records. Nor is there any species of writing, perhaps, upon the whole, more interesting, instructive, or impressive. Example proves the practicability of things, which the reasoning of the flesh would represent as unattainable; and conveys reproof in a language which, while it provokes to emulation, is incapable of giving offence. We may add, that, as things approach to our own situation and circumstances, they become more affecting: the life of one of your own sex, therefore, taken principally from her own diary, will, we presume, be read by you with increasing interest.

It affords us pleasure to compare female excellence as formed on the principles of revelation, with that which is formed on the principles of heathen or deistical philosophy. You may see in the hidden

---

[5] See Galatians 3:28.

To the Christian Females

moralist accounts of the virtues of women: but what are they? Accounts of women who have made brilliant sallies of wit, performed masculine feats for their country, and formed desperate resolutions to kill themselves rather than be enslaved. And this is the only kind of virtue inspired by the modern infidel philosophy, which, in fact, is not virtue. The best part of it is near natural accomplishment; and much of it is base and vicious. There is nothing in it of that pure chastity, of that sweet modesty; or, as a Scriptures term it, shamefacedness, which courts not to be seen; of that meekness, mildness, gentleness, sympathy, and goodness, which is the ornament of human nature, and the peculiar glory of women.

God has lately furnished us with a lovely example of pure, practical Christianity, in one of your sex, of splendid talents. Here you will see the same thing in one of yours in a more private station. We cannot but consider Miss Anthony as a female Pearce,[6] and not inferior to him in spirituality. The violet, though less conspicuous, is not less fragrant nor beautiful than the rose. A little maid of Israel, who was carried captive into Syria, recommended her master to a prophet, by whose means he was accused of his leprosy, and brought to acknowledge the God of Israel.[7] The chaste conversation of Christian females, presented as accomplishing that which the preaching of the Word itself did not accomplish.

Nor are such examples peculiar to the primitive times. Christianity produces the same affects, for substance, in all ages. The late Dr. Gibbons has done an important service to the church, by publishing *Memoirs of Eminently Pious Women*, in two volumes.[8] Such lives ought not to be lost to posterity: yet, the examples which he has

---

[6] Samuel Pearce (1766–1799), pastor of Cannon Street Baptist Church, Birmingham, and a close friend of Fuller, who regarded him as a model of Evangelical piety.

[7] The account of Naaman, his wife's Israelite servant girl, and the prophet Elisha is found in 2 Kings 5.

[8] Thomas Gibbons (1720–1785) was a Nonconformist author, whose two-volume Memoirs of Eminently Pious Women was published in 1777.

selected, are chiefly, if not wholly confined to persons of exalted rank; whose general deportment, of course, is beyond the reach of ordinary imitation. There is, no doubt, as great eminency in godliness to be found in the common walks of life, as in the higher circles. These were the walks which our Redeemer himself condescended to occupy, when upon earth; and it is pleasant to reflect that there is no station so humble as to incapacitate us for glorifying his name, or so obscure as to render ass beneath his notice.

A very interesting anecdote is related by a gentleman, who lately visited the north of Ireland, of the influence which the religion of a servant-maid had upon a whole family, in that country.

> The family (he says) were Dissenters: but, Dissenter, in many parts of Ireland, is but another name for an Arian or Socinian. The poor girl was much ridiculed for her religion, by the young ladies; but did not render evil for evil. On the contrary, she would allow them to laugh at her, and then mildly reason with them. She made it her study to be attentive and useful to them; took opportunities to speak to them about religion; and would offer to read the sacred scriptures to them when they went to bed. They commonly fell asleep, and that in a little time, under the sound; but she was not discouraged. Having exemplified Christianity in her life, the Lord sent a fever to call her home to himself. The young ladies were not permitted to see her during her illness; but they heard of her behaviour, which did not lessen the impression with her previous conduct had made upon them. Soon after, the two eldest began to make a profession of real religion. The little leaven spread; and now all the nine young ladies appear truly pious. Nor is religion, in this highly favoured family, confined to them; other means were employed by God, in producing a great change, but one of the two, who first became serious, informed me, that she chiefly ascribed it to the life and death of a servant-maid.

To the Christian Females

In the late extraordinary exertions for importing the gospel to the heathen,[9] your sex has borne an honourable part. They have not only generously contributed of the substance, and been unweariedly assiduous in accommodating those who have embarked in the important undertaking; but many of them have cheerfully left their country and their kindred, and, with their husbands, encountered its perils. Nor have they been less useful in their spheres of action than their companions.

Invading the lives of the most eminent Christians, we shall perceive a considerable variety; owing not only to the diversity of constitution, and religious advantages, but even to God's different manner of working upon different persons. This may instruct us not to set up the form and order of the experience of anyone, as a model by which to judge concerning those of others. We shall also perceive a degree of contrariety between the views and feelings of different persons whose Christianity nevertheless we cannot justly call in question. The doctrine with which we are most conversant at the time of our religious concern, whether by means of reading, hearing, or conversation, will insensibly give a colour not only to our language, but to the thoughts and feelings of our mind. It is thus that we could account for many differences which unhappily subsist among real Christians; and thus we acknowledge, we do account for what Miss Anthony says of a "sprinkling" being "the scriptural mode of baptism." We would however by no means disguise our opinion by striking out an expression which does not accord with our own convictions. And it is pleasant to add that while we perceive not only varieties, but contrarieties in the views and feelings even of eminent Christians, the former are but as the various features and the latter of the accidental spots in the human countenance. The great and

---

[9] The Baptist Missionary Society, which had been formed in 1792 and of which Fuller was the general secretary from 1792 till his death in 1815, was supported financially and prayerfully by women. A few of these women went abroad with their husbands as missionaries.

essential principles of Christianity are found in every Christian, no less than the distinguishing properties of humanity are found in every man.

No serious Christian, we apprehend, can read the life of Miss Anthony without receiving the sweetness and importance of heavenly things; and but few, if any, without being convinced by it of their own defects. It affords a singular specimen of the powerful influence of evangelical principles upon the heart and life, which, while it brings home to the bosom a proof of their divinity, must provoke the Christian reader to emulate the same holy and happy attainments, walking by the same rule, and minding the same thing.

John Ryland, D. D.
Andrew Fuller
John Sutcliff

Questions

1. What is "one of the glories of Christianity"? What is the biblical support for this assertion? How do Ryland, Fuller, and Sutcliff understand this assertion as it relates to women?
2. Why have Ryland, Fuller, and Sutcliff supported the publication of the *Memoirs of Miss Susanna Anthony*? How do they hope that the reader will be transformed by the reading of this work?
3. What do Ryland, Fuller, and Sutcliff see as the difference between secular models of femininity and Christian ones? Do you agree with them? Why or why not?
4. Use the internet to discover who Samuel Pearce (1766–1799) was or read the introduction to Michael A.G. Haykin, *Joy unspeakable and full of glory: The piety of Samuel and Sarah Pearce* (Kitchener, ON: Joshua Press, 2012).
5. What is being said by this comparison in this text: "The violet, though less conspicuous, is not less fragrant nor beautiful than the rose"? What does this tell you about the view of Ryland, Fuller, and Sutcliff about women?
6. What criticism do Ryland, Fuller, and Sutcliff have for Thomas Gibbons' two-volume *Memoirs of Eminently Pious Women*?
7. What role have women had in the ministry of the Baptist Missionary Society?
8. How do Ryland, Fuller, and Sutcliff explain the differences between "the most eminent Christians"? How do you think such differences ought to be viewed? But should we even have a category like "eminent Christians"? Why or why not?
9. What do Ryland, Fuller, and Sutcliff anticipate will be the impact of reading this *Memoirs of Miss Susanna Anthony*? In making these comments, what do Ryland, Fuller, and Sutcliff assume to be true of reading?

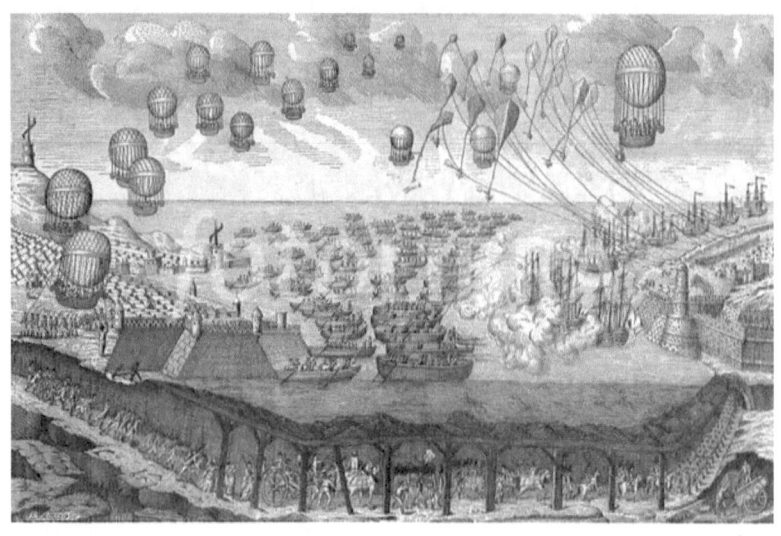

A contemporary depiction of Napoleon Bonaparte's intended invasion of Great Britain (the Channel tunnel and the balloons were actually suggested!)

9
Christian Patriotism; or the Duty of Religious People Towards Their Country[1] (1803)

Introduction

The outbreak of the French Revolution in 1789 led to an entire generation of war, as the French exported "unprecedented destruction and warfare"[2] to the rest of Europe, and so plunged the continent into a series of wars that more or less lasted until 1815. Not long before Fuller's delivery of *Christian Patriotism*, the treaty of Amiens (March 27, 1802), which had secured an uneasy peace in Europe for close to fourteen months, collapsed as open hostilities resumed between France and Great Britain. Almost immediately Napoleon Bonaparte (1769-1821) and his French generals committed themselves to extensive preparations for the invasion of England. Although these preparations would occupy much of Napoleon's energy for the next two years, events were at their most critical during the latter months of 1803, when invasion seemed an imminent certainty. Fuller's sermon, based upon Jeremiah 29:7—"Seek the peace of the city whither I have caused you to be carried away captives, and pray unto the Lord for it; for in the peace thereof shall ye have peace" (KJV)—sought to help the members of his congregation determine their Christian duty during a time of grave national crisis.

---

[1] From *The Complete Works of the Rev. Andrew Fuller*, ed. Joseph Belcher (1845, Harrisonburg, VA: Sprinkle Publications, 1988), I, 202-209.

[2] These words are those of Mark A. Noll in his discussion of the French Revolution as a turning-point in the history of Christianity: *Turning Points: Decisive Moments in the History of Christianity* (Grand Rapids, MI: Baker Books, 1997), 251.

The reader should not overlook Fuller's reference in this sermon to the evil of Britain's involvement in the slave trade. Along with a number of fellow Baptists like his friend William Carey (1761–1834), Fuller longed for the end of this vile iniquity. He lived to see the end of the slave trade in the British Empire in 1807, but slavery persisted down to 1833.

Christian Patriotism

> "And seek the peace of the city whither I have caused you to be carried away captives, and pray unto the Lord for it; for in the peace thereof shall ye have peace."[3]

In the course of human events, cases may be expected to occur in which a serious mind may be at a loss with respect to the path of duty. Presuming, my brethren, that such may be the situation of some of you, at this momentous crisis—a crisis in which your country, menaced by an unprincipled, powerful, and malignant foe, calls upon you to arm in its defense—I take the liberty of freely imparting to you my sentiments on the subject.

When a part of the Jewish people were carried captives to Babylon, ten years, or thereabouts, before the entire ruin of the city and temple, they must have felt much at a loss in determining upon what was duty. Though Jeconiah, their king, was carried captive with them, yet the government was still continued under Zedekiah; and there were not wanting prophets, such as they were, who encouraged in them the hopes of a speedy return. To settle their minds on this subject, Jeremiah, the prophet, addressed the following letter to them, in the name of the Lord:

---

[3] Jeremiah 29:7.

CHRISTIAN PATRIOTISM

Thus saith the Lord of hosts, the God of Israel, unto all that are carried away captives, whom I have caused to be carried away from Jerusalem unto Babylon; Build ye houses, and dwell in them; and plant gardens, and eat the fruit of them; take ye wives, and beget sons and daughters; and take wives for your sons, and give your daughters to husbands, that they may bear sons and daughters; that ye may be increased there, and not diminished: and seek the peace of the city whither I have caused you to be carried away captives, and pray unto the Lord for it; for in the peace thereof shall ye have peace.[4]

I do not suppose that the case of these people corresponds exactly with ours; but the difference is of such a nature as to heighten our obligations. They were in a foreign land; a land where there was nothing to excite their attachment, but everything to provoke their dislike. They had enjoyed all the advantages of freedom and independence, but were now reduced to a state of slavery. Nor were they enslaved only: to injury was added insult. They that led them captive required of them mirth, saying, "Sing us one of the songs of Zion!"[5] Revenge, in such circumstances, must have seemed natural; and if a foreign invader, like Cyrus, had placed an army before their walls, it had been excusable, one would have thought, not only to have wished him success, but if an opportunity had offered, to have joined an insurrection in aid of him yet nothing like this is allowed. When Cyrus actually took this great city, it does not appear that the Jews did any thing to assist him. Their duty was to seek the welfare of the city, and to pray to the Lord for it, leaving it to the great disposer of all events to deliver them in his own time; and this not merely as being right, but wise: "In their peace ye shall have peace."

Now if such was the duty of men in their circumstances, can there be any doubt with respect to ours? Ought we not to seek the good of

---

[4] Jeremiah 29:4-7.
[5] Psalm 137:3.

our native land; the land of our fathers' sepulchres; a land where we are protected by mild and wholesome laws, administered under a paternal prince; a land where civil and religious freedom are enjoyed in a higher degree than in any other country in Europe; a land where God has been known for many centuries as a refuge; a land, in fine, where there are greater opportunities for propagating the gospel, both at home and abroad, than in any other nation under heaven? Need I add to this that the invader was to them a deliverer; but to us, beyond all doubt, would be a destroyer?

Our object, this evening, will be partly to inquire into the duty of religious people towards their country, and partly to consider the motive by which it is enforced.

I. Inquire into the duty of religious people towards their country. Though, as Christians, we are not of the world, and ought not to be conformed to it; yet, being in it, we are under various obligations to those about us. As husbands, wives, parents, children, masters, servants, &c., we cannot be insensible that others have a claim upon us, as well as we upon them; and it is the same as members of a community united under one civil government. If we were rulers, our country would have a serious claim upon us as rulers; and, as we are subjects, it has a serious claim upon us as subjects. The manner in which we discharge these relative duties contributes not a little to the formation of our character, both in the sight of God and man. The directions given to the Jewish captives were comprised in two things: "seeking the peace of the city," and "praying to the Lord for it." These directions are very comprehensive; and apply to us, as we have seen, much more forcibly than they did to the people to whom they were immediately addressed. Let us inquire, more particularly, what is included in them.

Seek the peace of the city. The term here rendered peace signifies not merely an exemption from wars and insurrections, but prosperity in general. It amounts, therefore, to saying, "Seek the good or

Christian Patriotism

welfare of the city." Such, brethren, is the conduct required of us, as men and as Christians. We ought to be patriots, or lovers of our country.

To prevent mistakes, however, it is proper to observe that the patriotism required of us is not that love of our country which clashes with universal benevolence, or which seeks its prosperity at the expense of the general happiness of mankind. Such was the patriotism of Greece and Rome; and such is that of all others where Christian principle is not allowed to direct it. Such, I am ashamed to say, is that with which some have advocated the cause of negro slavery. It is necessary, forsooth, to the wealth of this country! No; if my country cannot prosper but at the expense of justice, humanity, and the happiness of mankind, let it be unprosperous! But this is not the case. Righteousness will be found to exalt a nation, and so to be true wisdom. The prosperity which we are directed to seek in behalf of our country involves no ill to any one, except to those who shall attempt its overthrow. Let those who fear not God, nor regard man, engage in schemes of aggrandizement, and let sordid parasites pray for their success. Our concern is to cultivate that patriotism which harmonizes with good-will to men. O my country, I will lament thy faults! Yet, with all thy faults, I will seek thy good; not only as a Briton, but as a Christian: "for my brethren and companions' sakes, I will say, 'Peace be within thee: because of the house of the Lord my God, I will seek thy good!' "[6]

If we seek the good of our country, we shall certainly do nothing, and join in nothing, that tends to disturb its peace, or hinder its welfare. Whoever engages in plots and conspiracies to overturn its constitution, we shall not. Whoever deals in inflammatory speeches, or in any manner sows the seeds of discontent and disaffection, we shall not. Whoever labours to depreciate its governors, supreme or subordinate, in a manner tending to bring government itself into

---

[6] Psalm 122:8.

contempt, we shall not. Even in cases wherein we may be compelled to disapprove of measures, we shall either be silent, or express our disapprobation with respect and with regret. A dutiful son may see a fault in a father; but he will not take pleasure in exposing him. He that can employ his wit in degrading magistrates is not their friend, but their enemy; and he that is an enemy to magistrates is not far from being an enemy to magistracy, and, of course, to his country. A good man may be aggrieved; and, being so, may complain. Paul did so at Philippi. But the character of a complainer belongs only to those who walk after their own lusts.

If we seek the good of our country, we shall do everything in our power to promote its welfare. We shall not think it sufficient that we do it no harm, or that we stand still as neutrals, in its difficulties. If, indeed, our spirits be tainted with disaffection, we shall be apt to think we do great things by standing aloof from conspiracies, and refraining from inflammatory speeches; but this is no more than may be accomplished by the greatest traitor in the land, merely as a matter of prudence. It becomes Christians to bear positive good-will to their country, and to its government, considered as government, irrespective of the political party which may have the ascendency. We may have our preferences, and that without blame; but they ought never to prevent a cheerful obedience to the laws, a respectful demeanour towards those who frame and those who execute them, or a ready co-operation in every measure which the being or well-being of the nation may require. The civil power, whatever political party is uppermost, while it maintains the great ends of government, ought, at all times, to be able to reckon upon religious people as its cordial friends; and if such we be, we shall be willing, in times of difficulty, to sacrifice private interest to public good; shall contribute of our substance without murmuring; and, in cases of imminent danger, shall be willing to expose even our lives in its defense.

Christian Patriotism

As the last of these particulars is a subject which deeply interests us at the present juncture, I shall be excused if I endeavour to establish the grounds on which I conceive its obligation to rest.

We know that the father of the faithful, who was only a sojourner in the land of Canaan, when his kinsman Lot with his family were taken captives by a body of plunderers, armed his trained servants, pursued the victors, and bravely recovered the spoil. It was on this occasion that Melchizedek blessed him, saying, "Blessed be Abraham of the most high God, possessor of heaven and earth: and blessed be the most high God, who hath delivered thine enemies into thine hand!"[7]

Perhaps it will be said, "This was antecedent to the times of the New Testament; Jesus taught his disciples not to resist evil; and when Peter drew his sword, he ordered him to put it up again; saying, 'All they that take the sword shall perish with the sword.'"[8]

You know, my brethren, I have always deprecated war, as one of the greatest calamities; but it does not follow, hence, that I must consider it in all cases unlawful.

Christianity, I allow, is a religion of peace; and whenever it universally prevails, in the spirit and power of it, wars will be unknown. But so will every other species of injustice; yet, while the world is as it is, some kind of resistance to injustice is necessary, though it may at some future time become unnecessary. If our Saviour's command that we resist not evil be taken literally and universally, it must have been wrong for Paul to have remonstrated against the magistrates at Philippi; and he himself would not have reproved the person who smote him at the judgment-seat.

I allow that the sword is the last weapon to which we should have recourse. As individuals, it may be lawful, by this instrument, to defend ourselves or our families against the attacks of an assassin; but,

---

[7] Genesis 14:9.
[8] Matthew 26:52.

perhaps, this is the only case in which it is so; and even there, if it were possible to disarm and confine the party, it were much rather to be chosen than in that manner to take away his life. Christianity does not allow us, in any case, to retaliate from a principle of revenge. In ordinary injuries it teaches patience and forbearance. If an adversary "smite us on the one cheek," we had better "turn to him the other also,"[9] than go about to avenge our own wrongs. The laws of honour, as acted upon in high life, are certainly in direct opposition to the laws of Christ; and various retaliating maxims, ordinarily practised among men, will no doubt be found among the works of the flesh.

And if, as nations, we were to act on Christian principles, we should never engage in war but for our own defense; nor for that, till every method of avoiding it had been tried in vain.

Once more, it is allowed that Christians, as such, are not permitted to have recourse to the sword, for the purpose of defending themselves against persecution for the gospel's sake. No weapon is admissible in this warfare but truth, whatever be the consequence. We may remonstrate, as Paul did at Philippi, and our Lord himself, when unjustly smitten; but it appears to me that this is all. When Peter drew his sword, it was with a desire to rescue his Master from the persecuting hands of his enemies, in the same spirit as when he opposed his going up to Jerusalem; in both which instances he was in the wrong: and the saying of our Saviour, that "all they that take the sword shall perish with the sword,"[10] has commonly been verified, in this sense of it.

I believe it will be found, that when Christians have resorted to the sword in order to resist persecution for the gospel's sake, as did the Albigenses, the Bohemians, the French Protestants,[11] and some

---

[9] Matthew 5:39.
[10] Matthew 26:52.
[11] The Albigensians were a thirteenth-century heretical sect derived from the Cathari, who held to a dualistic worldview. Fuller appears to have believed that they were orthodox.

CHRISTIAN PATRIOTISM

others, within the last six hundred years, the issue has commonly been, that they have perished by it; that is, they have been overcome by their enemies, and exterminated: whereas, in cases where their only weapons have been "the blood of the Lamb, and the word of their testimony, loving not their lives unto death,"[12] they have overcome. Like Israel in Egypt, the more they have been afflicted, the more they have increased.

But none of these things prove it unlawful to take up arms as members of civil society, when called upon to do so for the defense of our country. The ground on which our Saviour refused to let his servants fight for him, that he should not be delivered into the hands of the Jews, was, that his was a kingdom "not of this world;"[13] plainly intimating that if his kingdom had been of this world, a contrary line of conduct had been proper. Now this is what every other kingdom is: it is right, therefore, according to our Lord's reasoning, that the subjects of all civil states should, as such, when required, fight in defense of them.

Has not Christianity, I ask, in the most decided manner recognised civil government, by requiring Christians to be subject to it? Has it not expressly authorized the legal use of the sword? Christians are warned that the magistrate "beareth not the sword in vain;" and that he is "the minister of God, a revenger, to execute wrath upon him that doeth evil."[14] But if it be right for the magistrate to bear the sword, and to use it upon evil-doers within the realm, it cannot be wrong to use it in repelling invaders from without; and if it be right on the part of the magistrate, it is right that the subject should assist him in it; for otherwise, his power would be merely nominal, and he would indeed "bear the sword in vain."

The Bohemians were the followers of Jan Hus (d.1415). The French Protestants were the Calvinistic Huguenots.
  [12] Revelation 12:11.
  [13] John 18:36.
  [14] Romans 13:4.

We have not been used, in things of a civil and moral nature, to consider one law as made for the religious part of a nation, and another for the irreligious. Whatever is the duty of one, allowing for different talents and situations in life, is the duty of all. If, therefore, it be not binding upon the former to unite in every necessary measure for the support of civil government, neither is it upon the latter; and if it be binding upon neither, it must follow that civil government itself ought not to be supported, and that the whole world should be left to become a prey to anarchy or despotism.

Further, if the use of arms were, of itself, and in all cases, inconsistent with Christianity, it were a sin to be a soldier: but nothing like this is held out to us in the New Testament. On the contrary, we there read of two believing centurions; and neither of them was reproved on account of his office, or required to relinquish it. We also read of publicans and soldiers who came to John to be baptized, each asking, "What shall we do?" The answer to both proceeds on the same principle: they are warned against the abuses of their respective employments; but the employments themselves are tacitly allowed to be lawful. To the one he said, "Exact no more than that which is appointed you;"[15] to the other, "Do violence to no man, neither accuse any falsely, and be content with your wages."[16] If either of these occupations had been in itself sinful, or inconsistent with that kingdom which it was John's grand object to announce, and into the faith of which his disciples were baptized, he ought, on this occasion, to have said so, or, at least, not to have said that which implies the contrary.

If it be objected that the sinfulness of war would not be so much at the door of the centurions and soldiers as of the government by whose authority it was proclaimed and executed, I allow there is considerable force in this; but yet, if the thing itself were necessarily, and

---

[15] Luke 3:13.
[16] Luke 3:14.

Christian Patriotism

in all cases, sinful, every party voluntarily concerned in it must have been a partaker of the guilt, though it were in different degrees.

But granting, it may be said, that war is not, in itself, necessarily sinful; yet it becomes so by the injustice with which it is commonly undertaken and conducted. It is no part of my design to become the apologist of injustice, on whatever scale it may be practised. But if wars be allowed to be generally undertaken and conducted without a regard to justice, it does not follow that they are always so; and still less that war itself is sinful. In ascertaining the justice or injustice of war, we have nothing to do with the motives of those who engage in it. The question is, whether it be in itself unjust? If it appeared so to me, I should think it my duty to stand aloof from it as far as possible.

There is one thing, however, that requires to be noticed. Before we condemn any measure as unjust, we ought to be in possession of the means of forming a just judgment concerning it.

If a difference arise only between five families, or two individuals, though every person in the neighbourhood may be talking and giving his opinion upon it; yet it is easy to perceive that no one of them is competent to pronounce upon the justice or injustice of either side, till he has acquainted himself with all the circumstances of the case, by patiently hearing it on both sides. How much less, then, are we able to judge of the differences of nations, which are generally not a little complex, both in their origin and bearings; and of which we know but little, but through the channel of newspapers and vague reports! It is disgusting to hear people, whom no one would think of employing to decide upon a common difference between two neighbours, take upon them to pronounce, with the utmost freedom, upon the justice or injustice of national differences. Where those who are constitutionally appointed to judge in such matters have decided in favour of war, however painful it may be to my feelings, as a friend of mankind, I consider it my duty to submit, and to think well of their decision, till, by a careful and impartial examination of the grounds of the contest, I am compelled to think otherwise.

After all, there may be cases in which injustice may wear so prominent a feature, that every thinking and impartial mind shall be capable of perceiving it; and where it does so, the public sense of it will and ought to be expressed. In the present instance, however, there seems to be no ground of hesitation. In arming to resist a threatened invasion, we merely act on the defensive; and not to resist an enemy, whose ambition, under the pretence of liberating mankind, has carried desolation wherever he has gone, were to prove ourselves unworthy of the blessings we enjoy. Without taking upon me to decide on the original grounds of the difference, the question at issue with us is, "Is it right that any one nation should seek absolutely to ruin another, and that other not be warranted, and even obliged, to resist it?" That such is the object of the enemy, at this time, cannot be reasonably doubted. If my country were engaged in an attempt to ruin France, as a nation, it would be a wicked undertaking; and if I were fully convinced of it, I should both hope and pray that they might be disappointed. Surely, then, I may be equally interested in behalf of my native land!

But there is another duty which we owe to our country; which is that we pray to the Lord for it. It is supposed that religious people are a praying people. The godly Israelites, when carried into Babylon, were banished from temple-worship; but they still had access to their God. The devotional practice of Daniel was well known among the great men of that city, and proved the occasion of a conspiracy against his life. King Darius knew so much of the character of the Jews as to request an interest in their prayers, in behalf of himself and his sons. My brethren, your country claims an interest in yours; and I trust that, if no such claim were preferred, you would, of your own accord, remember it.

CHRISTIAN PATRIOTISM

You are aware that all our dependence, as a nation, is upon God; and, therefore, should importune his assistance. After all the struggles for power, you know that in his sight all the inhabitants of the world are reputed as nothing: he doth according to his will in the army of heaven, and among the inhabitants of the earth; and none can stay his hand, or say unto him, "What doest thou?" Indeed this has been acknowledged, and at times sensibly felt, by irreligious characters; but in general the great body of a nation, it is to be feared, think but little about it. Their dependence is upon an arm of flesh. It may be said, without uncharitableness, of many of our commanders, both by sea and land, as was said of Cyrus, God hath girded them, though they have not known him. But by how much you perceive a want of prayer and dependence on God in your countrymen, by so much more should you be concerned, as much as in you lies, to supply the defect. "The prayer of a righteous man availeth much."[17]

You are also aware, in some measure, of the load of guilt that lies upon your country; and should therefore supplicate mercy on its behalf. I acknowledge myself to have much greater fear from this quarter than from the boasting menaces of a vain man. If our iniquities provoke not the Lord to deliver us into his hand, his schemes and devices will come to nothing. When I think, among other things, of the detestable traffic before alluded to, in which we have taken so conspicuous a part, and have shed so much innocent blood, I tremble! When we have fasted and prayed, I have seemed to hear the voice of God, saying unto us, "Loose the bands of wickedness, undo the heavy burdens, let the oppressed go free, and break every yoke!"[18] Yet, peradventure, for his own name's sake, or from a regard to his own cause, which is here singularly protected, the Lord may hearken to our prayers, and save us from deserved ruin. We

---

[17] James 5:16.
[18] Isaiah 58:6.

know that Sodom itself would have been spared if ten righteous men could have been found fit her. I proceed to consider,

II. The motive by which these duties are enforced: "In the peace thereof shall ye have peace."[19]

The Lord hath so wisely and mercifully interwoven the interests of mankind as to furnish motives to innumerable acts of justice and kindness. We cannot injure others, nor even refrain from doing them good, without injuring ourselves.

The interests of individuals and families are closely connected with those of a country. If the latter prosper, generally speaking, so do the former; and if the one be ruined, so must the other. It is impossible to describe, or to conceive beforehand, with any degree of accuracy, the miseries which the success of a foreign enemy, such as we have to deal with, must occasion to private families. To say nothing of the loss of property among the higher and middle classes of people (which must be severely felt, as plunder will, undoubtedly, be the grand stimulus of an invading army), who can calculate the loss of lives? Who can contemplate, without horror, the indecent excesses of a victorious, unprincipled, and brutal soldiery? Let not the poorest man say, "I have nothing to lose." Yes, if men of opulence lose their property, you will lose your employment. You have also a cottage, and perhaps a wife and family, with whom, amidst all your hardships, you live in love; and would it be nothing to you to see your wife and daughters abused, and you yourself unable to protect them, or even to remonstrate, but at the hazard of being thrust through with the bayonet? If no other considerations will induce us to protect our country, and pray to the Lord for it, our own individual and domestic comfort might suffice.

To this may be added, our interests as Christians, no less than as men and as families, are interwoven with the well-being of our country. If Christians, while they are in the world, are, as has been already

---

[19] Jeremiah 29:7.

Christian Patriotism

noticed, under various relative obligations, it is not without their receiving, in return, various relative advantages. What those advantages are we should know to our grief, were we once to lose them. So long have we enjoyed religious liberty in this country, that I fear we are become too insensible of its value. At present we worship God without interruption. What we might be permitted to do under a government which manifestly hates Christianity, and tolerates it even at home only as a matter of policy, we know not. This, however, is well known, that a large proportion of those unprincipled men, in our own country, who have been labouring to overturn its constitution, have a deep-rooted enmity to the religion of Jesus. May the Lord preserve us, and every part of the united kingdom, from their machinations!

Some among us, to whatever extremities we may be reduced, will be incapable of bearing arms; but they may assist by their property, and in various other ways: even the hands of the aged poor, like those of Moses, may be lifted up in prayer; while their countrymen, and it may be their own children, are occupying the post of danger. I know it is the intention of several whom I now address freely to offer their services at this important period. Should you, dear young people, be called forth in the arduous contest, you will expect an interest in our prayers. Yes, and you will have it. Every one of us, every parent, wife, or Christian friend, if they can pray for any thing, will importune the Lord of Hosts to cover your heads in the day of battle!

Finally, it affords satisfaction to my mind to be persuaded that you will avail yourselves of the liberty granted to you of declining to learn your exercise on the Lord's day. Were you called to resist the landing of the enemy on that day, or any other work of necessity, you would not object to it; but, in other cases, I trust, you will. "Render to Caesar the things that are Caesar's, and unto God the things that are God's."[20]

---

[20] Mark 12:17.

Questions

1. Outline in a paragraph the situation facing England in 1803, when Andrew Fuller preached the sermon *Christian Patriotism*. To answer this question you will need to research the answer outside of Fuller's works.
2. What did God encourage the Israelites to do when they were taken into captivity by the Babylonians?
3. What application does Fuller make to his own day of this fact? In other words, what did Fuller see as a Christian duty vis-à-vis the British government?
4. Fuller asserts that "Christianity ... is a religion of peace." As such, what are the circumstances in which a Christian should never take up arms?
5. Are there circumstances in which a Christian can resort to arms? How does Fuller demonstrate this from the Scriptures? Do you agree with him? Why or why not?
6. Is Fuller right that our Lord's statement in the Sermon on the Mount that "we resist not evil" should not "be taken literally and universally"? Explain.
7. Fuller believes that "war is not, in itself, necessarily sinful." Does this mean that he is in favor of every military enterprise his nation might get involved in? What about the then-present war with France—is he in favor of that? Why?
8. What other duty does a Christian owe to his government?
9. What does Fuller mean when he says that he has greater fears about the "load of guilt" lying upon Great Britain than "the boasting menaces of a vain man"? Who is the "vain man" he is thinking of?
10. What other reasons would necessitate a Christian to take up arms?

Andrew Fuller's desk in Fuller Baptist Church, Kettering

10
An Essay on Truth: Containing an Inquiry into Its Nature and Importance[1] (1805)

Introduction

This essay originally appeared as an introduction to the British edition of Hannah Adams, *A View of Religions* (London: W. Button & Son, 1805), which was based on the third American edition (October, 1801). It reveals Fuller at his best as a theologian, arguing for both the existence of truth and its importance for human life. Although this text was written over two hundred years ago, Fuller's arguments for the reality of truth and its vital necessity for human flourishing are as pertinent now in our post-modern malaise as they were in his day. The concluding section of the essay, in which Fuller examines the nature of error and its origin, has been omitted.

An Essay on Truth

The multifarious and discordant sentiments which divide mankind afford a great temptation to scepticism, and many are carried away by it. The open enemies of the gospel take occasion from hence to justify their rejection of it; and many of its professed friends have written as if they thought that to be decided amidst so many minds and opinions were almost presumptuous. The principal, if not the only, use which they would make of these differences is to induce a spirit of moderation and charity, and to declaim against bigotry.

---

[1] From *The Complete Works of the Rev. Andrew Fuller*, ed. Joseph Belcher (1845, Harrisonburg, VA: Sprinkle Publications, 1988), III, 524–532. See also Andrew Fuller, *What Is Truth?* (Peterborough, ON: H&E Publishing, 2018).

To say nothing at present how these terms are perverted and hackneyed in a certain cause, let two things be seriously considered: First, whether this was the use made by the apostles of the discordant opinions which prevailed in their times, even among those who "acknowledged the divinity of our Saviour's mission?" In differences among Christians which did not affect the kingdom of God, nor destroy the work of God, it certainly was; such were those concerning meats, drinks, and days, in which the utmost forbearance was inculcated.[2] But it was otherwise in differences which affected the leading doctrines and precepts of Christianity. Forbearance in these cases would, in the account of the sacred writers, have been a crime. Paul would they were even cut off who troubled the Galatian churches by corrupting the Christian doctrine of justification.[3] And it is recorded to the honour of the church at Ephesus, that it "could not bear" them that were evil; but "had tried them who said they were apostles and were not, and found them liars."[4]

Secondly, whether an unfavourable opinion of those who reject what we account the leading principles of Christianity, supposing it to be wrong, be equally injurious with a contrary opinion, supposing that to be wrong? To think unfavourably of another does not affect his state towards God: if, therefore, it should prove to be wrong, it only interrupts present happiness. We have lately been told indeed, but from what authority I cannot conceive, that "the readiest way in the world to thin heaven, and to replenish the regions of hell, is to call in the spirit of bigotry." Far be it from me to advocate the cause of bigotry, or to plead for a bitter, censorious spirit, a spirit that would confine the kingdom of heaven to a party; but I do not perceive how this spirit, bad as it is, is productive of the effects ascribed to it. If, on the other hand, through an aversion to bigotry, we treat

---

[2] Romans 14:17, 20.
[3] Galatians 5:12.
[4] Revelation 2:2.

those as Christians to whom an apostle would at least have said, "I stand in doubt of you,"[5] we flatter and deceive them; which is really "the readiest way in the world to win heaven, and to replenish the regions of hell."

Surely there is a medium between bigotry and esteeming and treating men as Christians irrespective of their avowed principles. Certainly a benevolent and candid treatment is due to men of all denominations; but to consider all principles as equally safe is to consider truth as of no importance.

Let us candidly inquire, Christian reader, whether, notwithstanding the diversity of sentiments in the Christian world, truth may not be clearly ascertained? Whether it be not of the utmost importance? Whether the prevalence of error may not be accounted for? And lastly, whether the wisdom as well as the justice of God may not be seen in his permitting it?

What is truth?

In attempting to answer this question, I desire to take nothing for granted but that Christianity is of God, and that the Scriptures are a revelation of his will. If Christianity be of God, and he has revealed his will in the Holy Scriptures, light is come into the world, though the dark minds of sinful creatures comprehend it not. It does not follow, because many wander in mazes of fruitless speculation, that there is not a way so plain that a wayfaring man, or one who "walketh in the truth,"[6] though a fool, shall not err. The numerous sects among the Greeks and Romans, and even among the Jews at the time of our Saviour's appearing, did not prove that there was no certain knowledge to be obtained of what was truth. Our Lord considered himself as speaking plainly, or he would not have asked the Jews as

---

[5] Galatians 4:20.
[6] 3 John 1:4.

he did, "Why do ye not understand my speech?"[7] The apostles and primitive believers saw their way plainly; and though we cannot pretend to the extraordinary inspiration which was possessed by many of them, yet if we humbly follow their light, depending on the ordinary teachings of God's Holy Spirit, we shall see ours.

Truth, we may be certain, is the same thing as what in the Scriptures is denominated "the gospel," "the common salvation,"[8] "the common faith,"[9] "the faith once delivered to the saints,"[10] "the truth as it is in Jesus,"[11] etc., and what this is may be clearly understood by the brief summaries of the gospel, and of the faith of the primitive Christians, which abound in the New Testament. Of the former, the following are a few of many examples:

- "God so loved the world, that he gave his only begotten Son, that whosoever believeth in him should not perish, but have everlasting life."[12]
- "The Son of man came to seek and to save that which is lost."[13]
- "I am the way, the truth, and the life: no man cometh unto the Father but by me."[14]
- "To him gave all the prophets witness, that through his name whosoever believeth in him shall receive remission of sins."[15]
- "We preach Christ crucified, unto the Jews a stumblingblock, and unto the Greeks foolishness; but unto them which are called, both Jews and Greeks, Christ, the power of God, and the wisdom of God."[16]

---

[7] John 8:43.
[8] Jude 3.
[9] Titus 1:4.
[10] Jude 3.
[11] Ephesians 4:21.
[12] John 3:16.
[13] Luke 19:10.
[14] John 14:6.
[15] Acts 10:43.
[16] 1 Corinthians 1:23.

- "I determined not to know any thing among you, save Jesus Christ and him crucified."[17]
- "Moreover, brethren, I declare unto you the gospel which I preached unto you, which also ye have received, and wherein ye stand; by which also ye are saved, if ye hold fast what I preached unto you, unless ye have believed in vain; for I delivered unto you first of all that which I also received, how that Christ died for our sins according to the Scriptures; and that he was buried, and that he rose again the third day, according to the Scriptures."[18]
- "This is a faithful saying, and worthy of all acceptation, that Christ Jesus came into the world to save sinners, of whom I am chief."[19]
- "This is the record, that God hath given to us eternal life, and this life is in his Son."[20]
- "Neither is there salvation in any other; for there is none other name under heaven given among men whereby we must be saved."[21]

If language has any determinate meaning, it is here plainly taught that mankind are not only sinners, but in a lost and perishing condition, without help or hope but what arises from the free grace of God, through the atonement of his Son; that he died as our substitute; that we are forgiven and accepted only for the sake of what he hath done and suffered; that in his person and work all evangelical truth concentrates; that the doctrine of salvation for the chief of sinners through his death was so familiar in the primitive times as to become a kind of Christian proverb, or saying; and that on our receiving and retaining this depends our present standing and final salvation. If this doctrine be received, Christianity is received; if not, the record

---

[17] 1 Corinthians 2:2.
[18] 1 Corinthians 15:1–3.
[19] 1 Timothy 1:15.
[20] 1 John 5:11.
[21] Acts 4:12.

which God hath given of his Son is rejected, and he himself treated as a liar.

When this doctrine is received in the true spirit of it, which it never is but by a sinner ready to perish, all those fruitless speculations which tend only to bewilder the mind will be laid aside; just as malice, and guile, and envies, and evil speakings are laid aside by him who is born of God. They will fall off from the mind, like the coat of the chrysalis, of their own accord. Many instances of this are constantly occurring. Persons who, after having read and studied controversies, and leaned first to one opinion and then to another, till their minds have been lost in uncertainty, have at length been brought to think of the gospel, not as a matter of speculation, but as that which seriously and immediately concerns them; and, embracing it as good news to them who are ready to perish, have not only found rest to their souls, but all their former notions have departed from them as a dream when one awaketh.

Corresponding with the brief summaries of the gospel are the concise accounts given of the *faith* of the primitive Christians:

- "Whosoever believeth that Jesus is the Christ is born of God."[22]
- "Who is he that overcometh the world, but he that believeth that Jesus is the Son of God?"[23]
- "If thou shalt confess with thy mouth the Lord Jesus, and believe in thine heart that God hath raised him from the dead, thou shalt be saved."[24]

The sacred writers did not mean, by this language, to magnify the belief of one or two divine truths at the expense of others; but to exhibit them as bearing an inseparable connexion; so that if these were

---

[22] 1 John 5:1
[23] 1 John 5:5.
[24] Romans 10:9.

truly embraced, the other would be certain to accompany them. They considered the doctrine of the person and work of Christ as a golden link, that would draw along with it the whole chain of evangelical truth. Hence we perceive the propriety of such language as the following: "He that hath the Son hath life; and he that hath not the Son hath not life;"[25] "Whosoever denieth the Son, the same hath not the Father."[26]

The doctrine and the faith of the primitive Christians were summarily avowed every time they celebrated the Lord's supper. The leading truth exhibited by that ordinance is the same which John calls "the record," namely, that "God hath given unto us eternal life, and this life is in his Son."[27] Under the form of a feast, of which we are invited to take, to eat, and to drink, are set forth the blessings of the New Testament, or covenant, and the medium through which they were obtained; namely, "the blood of Jesus, shed for many for the remission of sins,"[28] and the way in which they must be received, that is to say, as a free gift, bestowed on the unworthy for his sake. If this simple doctrine were believed with the spirit of a little child, and lived upon as our meat and drink, we might take an everlasting leave of speculations on things beyond our reach; and that without sustaining the loss of anything but what were better lost than retained.

Importance of truth

If the above remarks may be thought sufficient to ascertain what is truth, its importance follows as a necessary consequence. If, as transgressors, we be exposed to the eternal displeasure of our Maker—if a door of hope be opened to us—if it be at no less an expense than the death of God's only begotten Son in our nature—if, through this great propitiation, God can be just, and the justifier of believers—

---

[25] 1 John 5:12.
[26] 1 John 2:23.
[27] 1 John 5:11.
[28] Matthew 26:28.

finally, if this be the only way of escape, and the present the only state in which it is possible to flee to it for refuge, who, that is not infatuated by the delusions of this world, can make light of it? There is an importance in truth, as it relates to philosophy, history, politics, or any other branch of science, inasmuch as it affects the present happiness of mankind; but what is this when compared with that which involves their everlasting salvation? To be furnished with an answer to the question, "What shall I do to be saved?"[29] is of infinitely greater account than to be able to decide whether the Ptolemaic or Copernican system be that of nature. The temporal salvation of a nation, great as it is, and greatly as it interests the minds of men, is nothing when compared with the eternal salvation of a single individual.

But many, who would not deny the superior value of eternal salvation to all other things, have yet gone about to depreciate the importance of divine truth, and to represent it as having no necessary connexion with either present holiness or future happiness. Such appears to have been the design of those well-known lines of Pope:

> For modes of faith let graceless zealots fight;
> His can't be wrong whose life is in the right.[30]

And to the same purpose we have often been told in prose that we shall not be judged at the last day by our opinions, but by our works. If truth and error existed in the mind merely as opinions, or objects of speculation, they might possibly have but little influence upon us; but if they be principles of action, they enter into the essence of all we do. Such is the influence of living faith, otherwise it could not be shown by our works; and such is that of the belief of falsehood, else

---

[29] Acts 16:30.
[30] This quote from Alexander Pope (1688-1744) is from his An Essay on Man, Epistle III, lines 305-306.

we had not read of the word of false teachers "eating as doth a gangrene."[31] The works by which we shall be judged cannot mean actions, in distinction from their principles, for as such they would contain neither good nor evil, but as connected with them. All pretences, therefore, to separate the one from the other are as contrary to reason as to Scripture.

To render this subject more evident, let the following particulars be duly considered:

First, it is by the belief of truth that sinners are brought into a slate of salvation. Great things are ascribed in the Scriptures to faith; but faith could have no existence without revealed truth as its foundation. Whatever importance, therefore, attaches to the one attaches to the other. The great blessing of justification is constantly ascribed to faith, not as the reward of a virtue, but as that by which we become one with Christ, and so partakers of his benefits. While unbelievers, we have no revealed interest in the divine favour; but are declared to be under condemnation; but, believing in him, we are no longer "under the law," as a term of life and death, but "under grace."[32] Hence it is that, in the gospel, as heard and received, we are said to stand. Take away evangelical truth, and you take away the standing of a Christian. Bereaved of this, the best man upon earth must despair of salvation.

Secondly, truth is the model and standard of true religion in the mind. That doctrines, whether true or false, if really believed, become principles of action—that they are a mould into which the mind is cast, and from which it receives its impression—is evident both from Scripture and experience. An observant eye will easily perceive a spirit which attaches to the different species of religion; and which, over and above the diversities arising from natural temper, will manifest itself in their respective followers. Paganism,

---

[31] 2 Timothy 2:17.
[32] Romans 6:14.

Mahomedism, Deism, apostate Judaism, and various systems which have appeared under the name of Christianity, have each discovered a spirit of its own. Thus, also it was from the beginning. Those who received another doctrine received with it another spirit; and hence we read of "the spirit of truth" and "the spirit of error." He that had the one is said to be "of God," and he that had the other "not of God."[33]

Revealed truth is represented as "a form of doctrine" into which believers are "delivered."[34] As a melted substance, cast into a mould, receives its form from it, and every line in the one corresponds with that of the other; so true religion in the soul accords with true religion in the Scriptures. Without this standard, we shall either model our faith by our own preconceived notions of what is fit and reasonable, or be carried away by our feelings, and lose ourselves among the extravagant vagaries of enthusiasm. Our views may seem to us very rational, or our feelings may be singularly ardent; and yet we may be far from being in the right. The question is, "Whether they agree line to line with the divine model?" God saith, in his Word, "Seek ye my face." If our hearts say unto him, "Thy face, Lord, will we seek,"[35] then does line answer to line; and this is true religion. Is it a leading feature of evangelical truth that it honours the divine character and government? It is the same with true religion in the mind. Does that manifest love even to enemies? So does this? Is it the object of the former to abase the pride of man? It is no less the nature of the latter to rejoice in lying low. Finally, is the one averse from all iniquity, and friendly to universal holiness? The other, dissatisfied with present attainments, "presseth towards the mark, for the prize of the high calling of God in Christ Jesus."[36]

---

[33] 2 Corinthians 11:4; 1 John 4:6.
[34] Romans 6:17.
[35] Psalm 27:8.
[36] Philippians 3:14.

Thirdly, truth is that which furnishes the motive for every exercise of true holiness. If once we are enabled to behold its glory, the glory of God in the face of Jesus Christ, it changes us into the same image, begets and excites holy affections, and every kind of gracious exercise. Hence we are said to *know* the truth, and the truth to make us free; to be sanctified through it, and begotten by it.[37]

It is not denied that there is much of what is called morality in persons who know and believe nothing to purpose of evangelical truth. Honour, interest, and the habits of education, will induce men to shun open immoralities, and to comply with things which are reputable and praiseworthy. But though there be great cause for thankfulness to God, who, by his providence, thus restrains mankind from much evil; yet this is not holiness. Holiness is the love of God and one another; whereas this is mere self-love. All works and worship of this kind are no better than the offering of Cain, which, being without faith, could not please God.

And as there may be a semblance of holiness without faith, so there may be a semblance of faith without holiness. The doctrines of the Bible, though in themselves practical, yet may be treated as mere speculations, and frequently are so by men who profess to believe them; and, where this is the case, instead of producing holiness, they may have a contrary effect: but this is owing to their being perverted. God's words do good to the upright. There is not a sentiment in the living oracles but what, if received in the true spirit and intent of it, will contribute to the sanctification of the mind.

True religion is, with great beauty and propriety, called walking in the truth. A life of sobriety, righteousness, and godliness, is Christian principle reduced to practice. Truth is a system of love, an overflow of the divine blessedness, as is intimated by its being called "the glorious gospel of the blessed God"[38]—a system of reconciliation,

---

[37] John 8:32; 17:17; James 1:18.
[38] 1 Timothy 1:11.

peace, and forgiveness; full of the most amazing condescension, and of spotless rectitude. To walk in truth like this is to walk in love, to be tender-hearted, forgiving one another, even as God for Christ's sake hath forgiven us; to be of the same mind with him who "made himself of no reputation, and took upon him the form of a servant;"[39] and "to be holy in all manner of conversation."[40]

Such were the fruits of truth which were actually brought forth by the primitive believers; and such, in different degrees, notwithstanding the many defects and scandals which abound among us, are the fruits of it in true Christians to this day. Thousands of examples, both in earlier and later times, might be produced, in which men who previously walked according to the course of this world, in rioting and drunkenness, in chambering and wantonness, in strife and envying, on embracing the doctrine of Christ crucified have put off all these, and become as it were new creatures.

It is also worthy of special notice, that, in every instance in which the primitive churches deviated from the doctrine of the apostles, they appear to have degenerated as to zeal and practical godliness. A careful review of the Epistles to the Corinthians, the Galatians, and the Hebrews, who departed more than any other churches from the simplicity of the gospel, would furnish proof of the justness of this remark. It was not without reason that Paul observed to the Corinthians, "evil communications corrupt good manners;"[41] by which he appears to have meant the communications of false teachers, who endeavoured to undermine the resurrection, and other important truths. And such was the corruption of manners which accompanied these notions, that, degenerate as we consider ourselves, compared with the primitive Christians, if any one of our churches tolerated the same things, we should be almost ready to pronounce it a

---

[39] Philippians 2:7.
[40] 1 Peter 1:15.
[41] 1 Corinthians 15:33.

synagogue of Satan. Among other things they divided into parties, boasted of the talents of their preachers, connived at the most unnatural kind of fornication, went to law with one another, communed with idolaters at their temples, and profaned the supper of the Lord by appropriating it to purposes of sensual indulgence! Such were the fruits of error.

If we look into the Epistle to the Galatians, who had been turned aside from the apostolic doctrine of justification, we shall find fruits of the same kind. They are described as not obeying the truth, as foolish, as in a manner bewitched; as having lost their former zeal, and rendered their Christianity a matter of doubt; as needing to have "Christ again formed in them," and it is strongly intimated that they were guilty of biting, and as it were *devouring* one another, of "fulfilling the lusts of the flesh," and of coveting "vain-glory, provoking one another, and envying one another."[42]

If the Hebrews had not, in turning aside from the truth, been injured in their spirit and conduct, it is very improbable that such language as the following would have been addressed to them:

> Wherefore, as the Holy Spirit saith, "Today, if ye will hear his voice, harden not your hearts, as in the provocation, in the day of temptation in the wilderness; when your fathers tempted me, proved me, and saw my works forty years. Wherefore I was grieved with that generation, and said, 'They do always err in their hearts, and they have not known my ways.' So I sware in my wrath, They shall not enter into my rest." Take heed, brethren, lest there be in any of *you* an evil heart of unbelief, in departing from the living God! Exhort one another daily, while it is called to-day, lest any of you be hardened through the deceitfulness of sin![43]

---

[42] See Galatians 3:1; 4:11, 19, 20; 5:7, 15, 16, 26.
[43] Hebrews 3:7-13.

Neither is it likely, if no symptoms had appeared among them, that they would have been exhorted to

> look diligently lest any man should fail of the grace of God; lest any root of bitterness springing up should trouble them, and thereby many be defiled; lest there should be any fornicator, or profane person, as Esau, who for one morsel of meat sold his birthright.[44]

Finally, it is not probable that so solemn a warning against whoredom and adultery would have been introduced, and the offenders cited as it were to the tribunal of God, if there had been no occasion for it in their own conduct.

Whether these instances of the pernicious effects of error in the primitive churches be not in direct opposition to the modern notions before stated, let the reader judge. Nor are such things peculiar to the primitive churches. If you see men desert the principles before stated, or hold them in a corrupted sense, you may commonly perceive a change in their spirit. They may retain what is called character, in the eyes of the world; but the savour of godliness is departed. They may retain their zeal; but it will be confined to some little peculiarity, to the neglect of the common faith. There will be a want of that lovely proportion which constitutes the true beauty of holiness. A man who chews opium, or tobacco, may prefer it to the most wholesome food, and may derive from it pleasure, and even vigour for a time; but his pale countenance, and debilitated constitution, will soon bear witness to the folly of spending his money for that which is not bread.

Fourthly, the love which the primitive Christians bore to one another was, for the truth's sake.[45] Now that for the sake of which we love a person is considered as of greater importance than any thing

---

[44] Hebrews 12:15–16.
[45] John 2; 3 John 1.

else pertaining to him. It is that which constitutes his value in our esteem; and which if he abandon, we should no longer esteem him.

Here we may perceive what is essential to the true legitimate charity of the primitive Christians. Instead of regarding men irrespectively of their principles, they "knew no man after the flesh."[46] John, who was the most loving, or charitable, perhaps, of all the disciples of Christ, is so far from considering a departure from the truth as a light matter, and the subject of it as entitled to the same Christian affection as heretofore, that he expressly writes as follows:

- Whosoever transgresseth, and abideth not in the doctrine of Christ, hath not God[47]
- If there come any unto you, and bring not this doctrine, receive him not into your house, neither bid him God speed; for he that biddeth him God speed is partaker of his evil deeds.[48]

Would not such language, I ask, in our days be reckoned very uncharitable? It would. But this proves, beyond all reasonable doubt, that the common ideas of charity are anti-scriptural. Charity will not take it for granted that whosoever deviates from our views must needs deviate from the doctrine of Christ; but will carefully inquire at the oracles of God, what is truth? Yet there is no need of being ever learning and never able to come to the knowledge of it. The lady whom John addressed was supposed to be able to distinguish between those who brought the doctrine of Christ and those who came without it; and so are Christians in the present day. Charity hopeth all things, and will always put the most favourable construction upon the motives of others that truth will admit; but without truth, as its ground and guide, it will not proceed.

---

[46] 2 Corinthians 5:16.
[47] 2 John 1:9.
[48] 2 John 9-10.

Here also we may see the nature of Christian unity. It is not merely for two or more persons to be agreed; for this they may be in evil. This is mere party attachment. It is natural for men to love those who think and act like themselves, and that for their own sake. But Christian unity is to love one another for Christ's sake, and for the truth's sake that dwelleth in them. Christ, as revealed in the gospel, forms the great point of union. A number of minds are drawn towards this point; and the nearer they approximate to it, the nearer they approach to a union with one another. If all true Christians were nearer to the mind of Christ, their differences would soon subside; and they would feel themselves, as they approached it, to be of one heart and of one soul.

Lastly, truth is the only solid foundation of peace and happiness. There are cases, it is granted, in which the mind may rejoice in error, or be distressed by truth. False doctrine will operate like opium, filling the imagination with pleasing dreams; but all is transient and delusive. Truth, on the other hand, when it barely commendeth itself to the conscience of a sinner, may render him extremely unhappy. Such was the effect of Judas's conviction of Christ's innocence; and such is the effect of similar convictions in the present times. But where truth takes possession of the heart—or, as the Scriptures express it, where we "receive the love of the truth"[49]—peace and joy accompany it. This is a fact established by history and experience, and is easily accounted for. Revealed truth carries in it a message of pardon, reconciliation, and eternal life; and all in a way honourable to the divine character and government. This, in itself, is good news; and to every one who, as a sinner ready to perish, receiveth it, is a source of solid and lasting happiness. Truth also pours light upon all the dark and mysterious events of time, and teaches us, while weeping over human misery, not to despond or repine; but, viewing things on a large scale, to rejoice in whatever is. It exhibits God upon the

---

[49] 2 Thessalonians 2:10.

throne of the universe, ordering every thing for the best; and thus reconciles the mind to present ill, by pointing it to the good that shall ultimately rise out of it.

Contrast with this the horrible complaints of an infidel:

> Who can, without horror, consider the whole earth as the empire of destruction? It abounds in wonders; it abounds also in victims; it is a vast field of carnage and contagion. Every species is, without pity, pursued and torn to pieces, through the earth, and air, and water! In man there is more wretchedness than in all other animals put together. He smarts continually under two sources which other animals never feel; anxiety, and listlessness in appetence, which makes him weary of himself. He loves life, and yet he knows that he must die. If he enjoy some transient good, for which he is thankful to heaven, he suffers various evils, and is at last devoured by worms. This knowledge is his fatal prerogative. Other animals have it not. He feels it every moment rankling and corroding in his breast. Yet he spends the transient moment of his existence in diffusing the misery which he suffers; in cutting the throats of his fellow creatures for pay; in cheating and being cheated; in robbing and being robbed; in serving, that he may command; and in repenting of all that he does. The bulk of mankind are nothing more than a crowd of wretches, equally criminal and unfortunate; and the globe contains rather carcasses than men. I tremble, upon a review of this dreadful picture, to find that it implies a complaint against providence; and I wish that I had never been born!

Such is the boasted happiness of unbelievers!

And though we should not go these lengths, yet, if we forsake truth, by deviating materially from any of the great doctrines of the gospel, it will affect our peace. Error is the wandering of the mind when it thinks without a guide; the issue of which is "stumbling upon the dark mountains." It is possible, in such circumstances, that the stupor of insensibility may be mistaken for the peace of God; but if the soul be once roused from its slumber, especially if it be the subject of any true religion, it will find itself miserable. As soon might we expect to find happiness in the mind of one who has lost its way, and knoweth not whither he goeth, as in a mind that has deviated from evangelical truth.

Questions

1. Why does Fuller believe that there is such a thing as truth?
2. What is the truth about the human condition according to Fuller and what has God done about it?
3. What does Fuller regard as the key doctrine of the Christian Faith?
4. What is the meaning of the Lord's Supper?
5. How does Fuller seek to bring home to his reader(s) the importance of truth at the beginning of this chapter?
6. What position does Fuller reject on and why?
7. What is the foundation of faith?
8. What is the relationship between doctrine and act in the Christian life? What does Fuller mean by the phrase "the extravagant vagaries of enthusiasm"?
9. What transforms "us into the same image [of Jesus Christ], begets and excites holy affections"?
10. "Truth is a system of love": what does Fuller mean by this statement?
11. Fuller states that some people in his day would regard the apostle John's words in 2 John 9-11 as "very uncharitable"—why? And why does Fuller think that such a sentiment is "anti-scriptural"?
12. What effects does false doctrine have? By contrast, what are the results of embracing truth?

The medallion that was struck for the 50th anniversary of the formation of the Baptist Missionary Society. Clockwise from the top it depicts the key founders of this society: Andrew Fuller, Samuel Pearce, John Sutcliff, John Ryland, and William Carey. The text surrounding this band of brothers is the motto of the Baptist Missionary Society, Zechariah 4:6: "Not by might, not by power, but my Spirit, saith the Lord."

11
The Promise of the Spirit, the Grand Encouragement in Promoting the Gospel[1] (1810)

Introduction

There is a deep vein of "loving study of the work of the Holy Spirit," to employ an expression of B.B. Warfield (1851-1921), traceable from the thought of the sixteenth-century Reformers through to that of their Puritan heirs in the following century and from thence to those Evangelicals, like Andrew Fuller, who were raised up in the eighteenth-century awakenings.[2] In this text, Fuller is particularly keen to emphasize the necessity of the Spirit's empowerment for mission. This text was originally penned as a circular letter for the Northamptonshire Association in 1810.

The Promise of the Spirit

Dear brethren,

In our last public letter, we addressed you on the work of the Holy Spirit;[3] in this we would direct your attention to the promise of the Spirit as the grand encouragement in promoting the spread of the gospel.

---

[1] From *The Complete Works of the Rev. Andrew Fuller*, ed. Joseph Belcher (1845, Harrisonburg, VA: Sprinkle Publications, 1988), III, 359-363.

[2] B.B. Warfield, "Introductory Note" to Abraham Kuyper, *The Work of the Holy Spirit* (1900, Grand Rapids, MI: Wm. B. Eerdmans Publ. Co., 1956), xxviii. For this pneumatological tradition, see also Richard B. Gaffin, "The Holy Spirit," *The Westminster Theological Journal* 43 (1980): 61; Garth B. Wilson, "Doctrine of the Holy Spirit in the Reformed Tradition: A Critical Overview" in George Vandervelde, ed., *The Holy Spirit: Renewing and Empowering Presence* (Winfield, BC: Wood Lake Books, 1989), 57-62.

[3] This circular letter had been penned by Robert Hall (1764-1831). See his "On the Work of the Holy Spirit" in *The Works of the Rev. Robert Hall, A.M.* (New York, NY: J. & J. Harper, 1832), I, 233-245

We take for granted that the spread of the gospel is the great object of your desire. Without this it will be hard to prove that you are Christian churches. An agreement in a few favourite opinions, or on one side of a disputed subject, or even a disagreement with others, will often induce men to form themselves into religious societies, and to expend much zeal and much property in accomplishing their objects; but this is not Christianity. We may be of what is called a sect, but we must not be of a sectarian spirit, seeking only the promotion of a party. The true churches of Jesus Christ travail in birth for the salvation of men. They are the armies of the Lamb, the grand object of whose existence is to extend the Redeemer's kingdom.

About eighteen years ago God put it into the hearts of a number of your ministers and members to do something for his name among the heathen; the effect of which has been to give an impulse to those labours for the attainment of the same object in our several stations at home. The success which has followed is sufficient to induce us to press forward in the work, and to search after every direction and every consideration that may aid our progress.

The influence of the Holy Spirit is by some disowned, by others abused; and even those who are the subjects of it, from various causes, enjoy much less of it than might be expected.

Those who disown it apply all that is said in the Scriptures on the subject to the communication of miraculous and extraordinary gifts, as though the Lord had long since forsaken the earth, and men were now to be converted by the mere influence of moral suasion. It is on this principle that writers, according to the leaning which they have felt towards the opinions of this or that political party, have represented the work of converting the heathen as either extremely easy or absolutely impossible. It is not for us to acquiesce in either; but, while we despair of success from mere human efforts, to trust in him who, when sending forth his servants to teach all nations, promised to be with them "to the end of the world."[4]

There are those, on the other hand, who abuse the doctrine, by converting it into an argument for sloth and avarice. God can convert sinners, say they, when he pleases, and without any exertions or contributions of ours. Yes, he can; and probably he will. Deliverance will arise from other quarters, and they who continue in this spirit will be destroyed!

Even those in whom the Spirit of God is enjoy much less of it[5] than might be expected; and this principally for want of the things which were stated in our letter of last year; namely, setting a proper value upon it, seeking it with fervent prayer, placing an entire dependence upon it, and maintaining a deportment suitable to it. In proving, therefore, that the promise of the Holy Spirit is the grand encouragement in promoting the spread of the gospel, we have not merely to oppose the adversaries of the doctrine, but to instruct and impress the minds of its friends. With these ends in view, let us recommend to your consideration the following remarks.

First, the success of God's cause under the Old Testament was considered by believers in those days as depending entirely upon God. God had a cause in the world from the earliest ages, and this it was which interested the hearts of his servants. It was for the setting up of his spiritual kingdom in the world that he blessed the seed of Abraham, and formed them into a people. This was the work that he carried on from generation to generation among them. When, therefore, sentence was passed on the people who came up out of Egypt, that they should die in the wilderness, Moses, who seems on that occasion to have written the 90th Psalm, was deeply concerned, lest, in addition to temporal judgments, the Lord should withdraw from them his Holy Spirit:

---

[4] Matthew 28:20.
[5] The use of "it" here is influenced by the KJV/AV: see, for example, Romans 8:16, 26.

> Let thy work, [said he] appear unto thy servants, and thy glory unto their children; and let the beauty of Jehovah our God be upon us: and establish thou the work of our hands upon us; the work of our hands establish thou it.[6]

It is worthy of notice that this prayer was answered. Though the first generation fell in the wilderness, yet the labours of Moses and his companions were blessed to the second. These were the most devoted to God of any generation that Israel ever saw. It was of them that the Lord said,

> I remember thee, the kindness of thy youth, the love of thine espousals, when thou wentest after me in the wilderness, in a land that was not sown. Israel was holiness unto the Lord, and the first-fruits of his increase.[7]

It was then that Balaam could not curse, but, though desirous of the wages of unrighteousness, was compelled to forego them, and his curse was turned into a blessing. We are taught by this case, amidst temporal calamities and judgments, in which our earthly hopes may be in a manner extinguished, to seek to have the loss repaired by spiritual blessings. If God's work does but appear to us, and our posterity after us, we need not be dismayed at the evils which afflict the earth.

Similar remarks might be made on the state of the church at the captivity. When the temple was burnt, and the people reduced to slavery in a foreign land, it must seem as if the cause of God in the world would go to ruin. Hence the prayer of Habakkuk: "O Lord, I have heard thy speech, and was afraid. O Lord, revive (or preserve alive) thy work in the midst of the years: in the midst of the years make known; in wrath remember mercy."[8] This prayer also was

---

[6] Psalm 90:16–17.
[7] Jeremiah 2:2–3.
[8] Habakkuk 3:2.

answered. The work of God did not suffer, but was promoted by the captivity. The church was purified, and the world, beholding the divine interposition, acknowledged, "The Lord hath done great things for them."[9]

After the return of the captives, they went about to rebuild the temple; but they had many adversaries, and no military force to protect them. On this occasion the prophet Zechariah (who with Haggai stood to strengthen the builders) had a vision. He saw, and behold,

> a candlestick, all of gold, with a bowl upon the top of it; and his seven lamps therein; and seven pipes to the seven lamps; and two olive trees on each side of the bowl, which, through the golden pipes, emptied the golden oil out of themselves.[10]

On inquiry of the angel what these meant, he was answered, "This is the word of the Lord unto Zerubbabel, saying, 'Not by might, nor by power, but by my Spirit,' saith the Lord of hosts."[11] As if he had said, This vision contains a message of encouragement to Zerubbabel, the purport of which is, Not by army or by power, etc. For, like as the candlestick is supplied without the hand of man, so God will prosper his cause, not by worldly power or armies, but by his gracious influence and superintending providence.

Here, also, a lesson is taught us, not to wait for legal protection, or even toleration, before we endeavour to introduce the gospel into a country; but to engage in the work, trusting in God, not only to succeed our labours, but, while acting on Christian principles, either to give us favour in the eyes of those with whom we have to do, or strength to endure the contrary.

Further, the success of the gospel in the times of the apostles is ascribed to the influence of the Holy Spirit, as its first or primary

---

[9] Psalm 126:3.
[10] Zechariah 4:2.
[11] Zechariah 4:6.

cause. That the truth of the doctrine, and even the manner in which it was delivered, contributed as second causes to its success, is allowed. Such appears to be the meaning of Acts 14:1, "They so spake that a great multitude believed." But if we look to either of these as the first cause, we shall be unable to account for the little success of our Lord's preaching when compared with that of his apostles. He spoke as never man spoke; yet compared with them he laboured in vain, and spent his strength for nought and in vain. It is the Holy Spirit to which the difference is ascribed. They did greater works than he, because, as he said, "I go to the Father."[12]

In promising to "be with his disciples to the end of the world,"[13] he could refer to no other than his spiritual presence; to this, therefore, he taught them to look for encouragement. To this cause the success of the apostles is uniformly ascribed:

- "The hand of the Lord was with them, and a great number believed, and turned to the Lord.[14]
- "God always causeth us to triumph in Christ, and maketh manifest the savour of his knowledge by us in every place."[15]
- "The Lord opened the heart of Lydia, and she attended unto the things which were spoken of Paul."[16]
- "The weapons of our warfare are mighty through God to the pulling down of strong holds."[17]

The great success which prophecy gives us to expect in the latter days is ascribed to the same cause. Upon the land of my people shall be thorns and briers "until the Spirit be poured upon us from on high."[18] Then the wilderness would be a fruitful field, and that which

---

[12] John 14:12.
[13] Matthew 28:20.
[14] Acts 11:21.
[15] 2 Corinthians 2:14.
[16] Acts 16:14.
[17] 2 Corinthians 10:4.
[18] Isaiah 32:15.

had been hitherto considered as a fruitful field would be counted a forest.

If the success of the gospel were owing to the pliability of the people, or to any preparedness, natural or acquired, for receiving it, we might have expected it to prevail most in those places which were the most distinguished by their morality, and most cultivated in their minds and manners. But the fact was, that in Corinth, a sink of debauchery, God had "much people;"[19] whereas in Athens, the seat of polite literature, there were only a few individuals who embraced the truth. Nor was this the greatest display of the freeness of the Spirit: Jerusalem, which had not only withstood the preaching and miracles of the Lord, but had actually put him to death—Jerusalem bows at the pouring out of his Spirit; and not merely the common people, but "a great company of the priests, were obedient to the faith."[20]

To the above may be added, the experience of those whose ministry has been most blessed to the turning of sinners to God. Men of light and speculative minds, whose preaching produces scarcely any fruit, will go about to account for the renewal of the mind by the established laws of nature; but they who see most of this change among their hearers see most of God in it, and have been always ready to subscribe to the truth of our Lord's words to Peter: "Flesh and blood hath not revealed it unto thee, but my Father who is in heaven."[21]

To this brief statement of the evidence of the doctrine, we shall only add a few remarks to enforce "the prayer of faith"[22] in your endeavours to propagate the gospel both at home and abroad. This is the natural consequence of the doctrine. If all our help be in God, to him it becomes us to look for success. It was from a prayer-meeting, held in an upper room, that the first Christians descended, and commenced that notable attack on Satan's kingdom in which three

---

[19] Acts 18:10.
[20] Acts 6:7.
[21] Matthew 16:17.
[22] James 5:13–16.

thousand fell before them. When Peter was imprisoned, prayer was made without ceasing of the church unto God for him. When liberated by the angel, in the dead of night, he found his brethren engaged in this exercise. It was in prayer that the late undertakings for spreading the gospel among the heathen originated. We have seen success enough attend them to encourage us to go forward; and probably if we had been more sensible of our dependence on the Holy Spirit, and more importunate in our prayers, we should have seen much more. The prayer of faith falls not to the ground. If "we have not," it is "because we ask not;" or, if "we ask and receive not," it is "because we ask amiss."[23] Joash smote thrice upon the ground and stayed, by which he cut short his victories. Something analogous to this may be the cause of our having no more success than we have.

Consider, brethren, the dispensation under which we live. We are under the kingdom of the Messiah, fitly called "the ministration of the Spirit," because the richest effusions of the Holy Spirit are reserved for his reign, and great accessions to the church from among the Gentiles ordained to grace his triumphs. It was fit that the death of Christ should be followed by the outpouring of the Spirit, that it might appear to be what it was, its proper effect; and that which was seen in the days of Pentecost was but an earnest of what is yet to come. To pray under such a dispensation is coming to God in a good time. In asking for the success of the gospel, we ask that of the Father of heaven and earth in which his soul delighteth, and to which he has pledged his every perfection; namely, to glorify his Son.

Finally, Compare the current language of prophecy with the state of things in the world, and in the church. In whatever obscurity the minutia of future events may be involved, the events themselves are plainly revealed. We have seen the four monarchies, or preponderating powers, described by Daniel as successively ruling the world; namely, the Babylonian, the Persian, the Macedonian, and the

---

[23] James 4:2–3.

Roman. We have seen the last subdivided into ten kingdoms, and the little papal horn growing up among them. We have seen the saints of the Most High "worn out" for more than a thousand years by his persecutions. We have seen his rise, his reign, and, in a considerable degree, his downfall. "The judgment is set," and they have begun to "take away his dominion;" and will go on "to consume and to destroy it unto the end."[24] And when this is accomplished, "the kingdom and dominion, and the greatness of the kingdom under the whole heaven, will be given to the people of the saints of the Most High."[25] It is not improbable that "the days of the voice of the seventh angel, when he shall begin to sound,"[26] have already commenced; which voice, while it ushers in the vials or seven last plagues upon the antichristian powers, is to the church a signal of prosperity: for, the seventh angel having sounded, voices are heard in heaven, saying, "The kingdoms of this world are become the kingdoms of our Lord and of his Christ; and he shall reign for ever and ever."[27] The glorious things spoken of the church are not all confined to the days of the millennium; many of them will go before it, in like manner as the victorious days of David went before the rest, or pacific reign, of Solomon, and prepared its way. Previous to the fall of Babylon, an angel is seen flying in the midst of heaven, having the everlasting gospel to preach to them that dwell on the earth; and before that terrible conflict in which the beast and the false prophet are taken, the Son of God is described as riding forth on a white horse, and the armies of heaven as following him. The final ruin of the antichristian cause will be brought upon itself by its opposition to the progress of the gospel.

The sum is, that the time for the promulgation of the gospel is come; and, if attended to in a full dependence on the promise of the

---

[24] Daniel 7:26.
[25] Daniel 7:27.
[26] Revelation 10:7.
[27] Revelation 11:15.

Spirit, it will, no doubt, be successful. The rough places in its way are smoothing, that all flesh may see the salvation of God. The greatest events pertaining to the kingdom of heaven have occurred in such a way—as to escape the observation of the unbelieving world, and, it may be, of some believers. It was so at the coming of our Lord, and probably will be so in much that is before us. If we look at events only with respect to instruments, second causes, and political bearings, we shall be filled with vexation and disquietude, and shall come within the sweep of that awful threatening, "Because they regard not the works of the Lord, nor the operations of his hands, he will destroy them, and not build them up."[28] But if we keep our eye on the kingdom of God, whatever become of the kingdoms of this world, we shall reap advantage from every thing that passes before us. God in our times is shaking the heavens and the earth: but there are things which cannot be shaken: "Wherefore we, receiving a kingdom which cannot be moved, let us have grace whereby we may serve God acceptably, with reverence and godly fear."[29]

---

[28] Psalm 28:5.
[29] Hebrews 12:28.

Questions

1. What does Fuller see as one evidence of true Christianity?
2. In the light of Particular Baptist experience in the eighteenth century, what is significant about Fuller's statement that "we may be of what is called a sect, but we must not be of a sectarian spirit"?
3. When Fuller describes local Baptist churches as "armies of the Lamb," what does this tell you about his ecclesiology?
4. What are two ways in which the work of the Spirit with regard to evangelism is abused?
5. Fuller mentions four reasons as to why "those in whom the Spirit is enjoy much less of it than might be expected." What are they? What does this section of this circular letter tell you about Fuller's purpose in writing it?
6. How does the Old Testament support Fuller's argument? How does he apply the Old Testament texts he cites to his own day?
7. What was the primary reason for the success of the gospel in the Apostolic Church? Detail the proof that Fuller gives for this assertion.
8. Is Fuller's statement that the Lord Jesus had "little success" compared to his apostles well-founded? Why or why not?
9. What does Fuller see as the practical conclusion of all that he has said to this point? What examples does he give to reinforce his point?
10. How does Fuller view Pentecost? Why will God give a favorable answer to those who pray for the conversion of the heathen? What does this tell you about his view of God?
11. In a version of this circular letter that the editor edited for *The Banner of Truth* magazine in November, 1986, he omitted the final two paragraphs of the letter as it was originally penned by

Fuller. Was he right to do so? What do they add to Fuller's argument?

George Charles Smith

12
On Being Missional—
a Letter to George Charles Smith[1]
(1811)

Introduction

George Charles Smith (1782–1863) had a noteworthy ministry among sailors and soldiers, but he was quite eccentric. He once referred to himself as "George Charles Smith BBU," that is, Burning Bush Unconsumed![2] Around 1810 he sought Fuller's advice on the formation of a society devoted to the evangelization of seamen. Fuller's reply below is a fabulous distillation of his thinking about how to do missions. Not surprisingly, in the course of the nineteenth-century British institutionalization of the missionary endeavour, Fuller's advice fell out of favour.

On Being Missional—a Letter to George Charles Smith

Kettering, January 1, 1811

My dear brother Smith:

The regard you have for the poor sailors endeared you to me. Indeed, I consider it as put into your heart by the Lord, and as betokening designs of mercy. It was probably for this purpose that

---

[1] This letter can be found in [George Charles Smith], "First Naval Mission, Andrew Fuller, Isaiah Birt, etc.," *The Mariners' Church Gospel Temperance Soldiers & Sailors' Magazine* [Supplement,] 28, no.12 (December, 1847): 4–7.

[2] "George Charles (Bo'sun) Smith 1782–1863," St. George-in-the-East (http://www.stgitehistory.org.uk/media/bosunsmith.html; accessed August 14, 2020). For his life, see Roald Kverndal, *George Charles Smith of Penzance: From Nelson Sailor to Mission Pioneer* (Littleton, CO: William Carey Library, 2012). See also Richard Blake, *Evangelicals in the Royal Navy 1775–1815: Blue Lights & Psalm-Singers* (Woodbridge, Suffolk: The Boydell Press, 2008), 232–237.

Providence placed you at sea in your earlier days. I give full credit to your account of the deplorable state of the navy, in a moral and religious view. The only question is, what are the best practicable means of ameliorating it! From the first mention of a society, I was struck with apprehension. Brother Greatheed was convinced that unless we could obtain authority sanctioning a person's going on board to distribute tracts, Bibles, etc. we could do nothing even were we to form a society.[3] But such an authority I am persuaded cannot be obtained; it may be done by connivance, just as we have obtained footing in India, but no otherwise. To form a society for the express purpose would defeat the end.

Being less acquainted with naval matters than those who reside at our principal sea-ports, I wrote to Mr. Birt as follows:

> I should expect such a society would raise a flame of persecution against the poor men from their officers; and, therefore, everything that is done, should be done in a still and quiet way, merely by individuals, who, whatever understanding they may have with each other, should not exist as a body. We know there is no part of the community so little at liberty as the army and navy; but the law allows them to write and receive letters from individuals on shore. This, therefore, is the door that is open; and if we go beyond it, may not this door some way be contrived to shut upon us? You, living at a sea-port, may be better able to give an opinion on this question than many others; I will, therefore, thank you for it.[4]

To this I have received an answer, as follows:

---

[3] Samuel Greatheed (1759-1823) was the rector at Bishops Hull, Somerset.

[4] Isaiah Birt (1758-1837) was the pastor of the Baptist church in Devonport. The Birmingham Congregationalist John Angell James (1785-1859) once said of him that he was "no ordinary man. His preaching was richly evangelical ... [and his] gift in prayer was extraordinary." Cited S. Pearce Carey, *Samuel Pearce, M.A., The Baptist Brainerd* [London: The Carey Press, 1913]), 59.

Your objections to a nautical society, and your plan of doing everything merely by individuals, meet my most perfect approbation. The navy and army are servants. Suppose a society formed to promote religion among the king's household servants, or servants in gentlemen's families, would it not be a high offence, and so defeat the end? We call it religion, but they would call it Methodism,[5] and set themselves against it; when, if only conducted by individuals, in a still way, the gospel might penetrate even to king's palaces.

I think I stated to brother Greatheed in my last, that I had written to William Wilberforce, Esq., M.P.,[6] copying the greater part of the letters from Hubback and Tooly,[7] and a part of Mr. Greatheed's to me, containing his proposals, and submitting a few questions upon them; to this I have received the following answers:

December 24th, 1810. I have received your most interesting letter, and will myself consider and consult with some friends as to the best course to be pursued for the attainment of the object, which must be dear to all who are interested for religion, and even for religious liberty. "December 25th. I am entirely of opinion, that if we were to form a society expressly for the purpose of carrying into effect the excellent suggestion of Mr. Greatheed (for whom, having had the pleasure of being introduced to him last summer, I need not say I feel a real esteem and regard), it would excite so much alarm as entirely to defeat the object. I doubt whether there be any better mode of proceeding than that of finding out some confidential and unexceptionable person at each of the great sea-ports, who might be supplied with tracts [and Bibles] by the three societies you mention, and by whom a communication might be obtained with the ships of war. But we must proceed very cautiously

---

[5] I.e., fanaticism.
[6] William Wilberforce (1759–1833), the Evangelical abolitionist.
[7] In a footnote, Fuller noted that these were the names of two "seamen, in different ships of war, who corresponded with me."

and circumspectly; and it is highly important that in all your communications on this subject you should enjoin the strictest secrecy. Perhaps it may be desirable to lose no time in endeavoring to find persons of the above description at the different sea-ports.

You allow that much noise would be made by the formation of a new society, and that considerable opposition might be expected, but think it would meet with so many advocates, and be an object so popular in the general, that nothing would ultimately defeat the grand object. That it might be popular, and meet with many advocates among religious people, I allow: I should not reckon, however, on universal approbation even there; for though it would not be a party business, yet there is so much of party spirit among religious people, that whoever took the lead, they would be suspected by others; and while some were zealous advocates, others would give a suspicious colouring to the whole. But allowing the utmost of your expectations, yet the whole body of religious people in the land are as nothing in comparison of the irreligious. Irreligious churchmen, irreligious Dissenters, and, what are more numerous that all others put together, irreligious absenters, form the bulk of the nation. This last description of men, I mean those who attend no worship in ordinary, abound in the legislature, and in all public offices, civil, military, or naval, and are always ready to use their utmost influence against religion, which they hate with a mortal hatred.

I remember, as may also brother Greatheed, that about the year 1787, when there were meetings all over the country for an application to Parliament for the repeal of the Corporation and Test Acts,[8]

---

[8] The Corporation and Test Acts had been passed in 1661 and 1673 respectively. The Corporation Act required, among other things, all magistrates, officers and members of municipal corporations to take an oath of allegiance to the crown and to affirm that in the preceding year they had received the Lord's Supper according to the rites of the Church of England. The Test Act, which was primarily aimed at Roman Catholics, required all officers who held civil or military posts to swear their allegiance to the crown, to partake of the Lord's Supper

great expectations were entertained from the popularity of the measure, and the advocates we should have in Parliament—as if reason were to prevail over interest. Some were so sanguine, if I remember right, as to intimate that Parliament dare not refuse us. The result was, however, that our strength, when weighted against that of our opponents, was weakness; and instead of gaining the object, we threw it at least half a century backwarder than it was when we began. The measure was popular, no doubt, among Dissenters, but unpopular with the irreligious.

My heart also revolts at all such plans and societies as are attended with parade. They do not appear to me to accord with the genius of that kingdom which cometh not with observation, or outward show; it was by a still, quiet, unostentatious process, that it was first obtained. The Pharisees demanded, when the kingdom of God should come? The answer of Jesus intimated that it would come without their seeing it, or being able to say where it was; nay, little as they might think of it, it was already amongst them.[9] Such appears to have been the process hitherto in the navy, and of the part that you have taken in it. One on board a ship is useful to another, and they to another, and so on. You found out individuals, and corresponded with them, and they brought you acquainted with others. On this principle, I should say, proceed. Find out suitable persons, one at each seaport, who would avail himself to ships coming in, to distribute tracts and Bibles, which he would receive of the society, all in a still, prudent, unostentatious way, neither blowing a trumpet before him, nor sounding it abroad in magazines or newspapers when it was done. Keep an account of all your expenses, and if good be done, the public will know it and repay you. Correspond as much as you are able with the ships, and engage other evangelical ministers

---

according to the rites of the established church and to deny the veracity of the Roman Catholic doctrine of transubstantiation. Both acts also discriminated against Dissenters, who sought to have them revoked in the late eighteenth century.

[9] See Luke 17:20-21.

of different denominations to do the same. According to the number of ships which admit of correspondence, such should be the number of correspondents. Three or four in aid of you would be sufficient at present. By this simple proceeding, it seems to me all the ends you propose might be answered, as well, if not better, than by the other; and this would be acting upon the principle which God hath already blessed.

A society on the plan you propose, seems to me an unwieldly, ostentatious affair, in which there would be great danger, at least, of miscarriage—of more attention being paid to the honour of the thing than to the thing itself—and of more time being taken up, and more money spent in adjustments, than in doing the work. You calculate upon the number of seamen, and the quantity of guilt and wretchedness among them, and wish for an institution that shall cover the whole at once. This is benevolent, but it is not God's usual way. When the world, after the flood, had all gone into idolatry, he could at once have met the tide, and turned it; but he called Abraham alone, and blessed him, and increased him, and said unto him, "I will bless thee, and thou shalt be a blessing."[10] The kingdom of heaven does not resemble the proposed siege of Hushai the Archite (a scheme not intended to succeed) in which all Israel were to bring ropes to the city, and draw it into the river, until there should not be one stone left upon another,[11] but is likened to a little leaven, hid in three measures of meal, till the whole was leavened.[12] I can see God's hand in what has been done hitherto; and I love to see it, rather than the hand of men.

It is one of Satan's devices, where he cannot quench the zeal of a servant of Christ, to turn it into a wrong direction. We have a missionary in the east, whose zeal was great, and I believe very

---

[10] Genesis 12:2.
[11] 2 Samuel 17:13.
[12] Matthew 13:33.

disinterested; but he had nearly been overset by this device. He was exceedingly dissatisfied with having only a few hundred of the New Testament in the language of the natives to distribute around his station, pleading the many millions of souls who were perishing round him for lack of knowledge (as though all had stood ready to read, and all Christendom had nothing but to furnish them with testaments) and unless he could meet the wants of all, he might as well do nothing. Thus, by aiming at things which are beyond reach, we may be in danger of neglecting those which are within reach.

After all, far be it from me to wish to govern you, or any of my brothers; I only show my opinion, and leave it. If you and others think it right to proceed on a different plan, do so; but I must be excused from having any concern in it. Indeed, I can only offer a little general advice upon any plan; for, partly owing to my inland situation, and partly to my numerous engagements in the Baptist Mission, it were impossible for me to carry on a new course of correspondence, either by sea or land. Good Mr. Hitchings, of Stoke, I know very well.[13] I am sorry that Lieut. Marks should think of going to sea no more. He seems to have been a blessing indeed on board the *Conqueror*.[14] I will mention what you say of the interference of government having an unhappy effect on captains, though I do not suppose any interference will be made by governments as such, nor in any other way than gentle recommendation.

---

[13] Otherwise unknown.
[14] The H.M.S. Conqueror had been built in 1800, saw action at the Battle of Trafalgar (1805), and was a ship of the line in the Royal Navy till 1821. See Robert Holden Mackenzie, *The Trafalgar Roll* (London: George Allen & Co., 1913), 147-150.

Richard Marks (1778-1847) was an enlisted seaman who rose through the ranks to become a master's mate on board the H.M.S. Defence, which also saw action at Trafalgar. His sterling conduct during that battle led to his promotion to lieutenant. In 1810 he left the Royal Navy to study theology at the University of Cambridge. He became curate of the Anglican parish at Waterbeach, Cambridgeshire, in 1812. Eight years later he was appointed vicar of Great Missenden, Buckinghamshire, where he served for 24 years. He was widely known for his robust Evangelical convictions, both during and after his service in the navy. See Blake, *Evangelicals in the Royal Navy*, 228-267.

May God direct your way. I am, my dear brother, affectionately yours, A. Fuller.

Questions

1. Read the entire letter and then answer this question: why does Fuller have serious misgivings about the formation of a society specifically designed to evangelize soldiers and sailors?
2. What has Samuel Greatheed suggested as an alternate plan of action?
3. How does the larger British world view the Christian Faith? How does Fuller know this?
4. What do these two statements tell you about Fuller's thinking about missions: a) "My heart also revolts at all such plans and societies as are attended with parade;" and b) "I can see God's hand in what has been done hitherto; and I love to see it, rather than the hand of men"?
5. What plan of action does Fuller suggest to Smith?

A stained-glass representation of Andrew Fuller
in Fuller Baptist Church, Kettering

Scripture Index

Old Testament

Genesis
  2:23 28
  3:4 78
  12:2 182
  14:9 131
  32:12 94
Deuteronomy
  29:19 78
  32:2 21
Joshua
  7:10–13 19
Judges
  5:23 26
  5:15–16 26
2 Samuel
  17:13 182
2 Kings
  19:28 42
2 Chronicles
  31:20–21 53
Ezra
  7:6 53
  7:10 53
  8:21 53
Nehemiah
  5:19 54
Psalms
  1:3 51
  24:7 90
  27:8 152
  28:5 172
  51:11 45
  90:16–17 166
  116:10 86
  122:8 129
  126:3 167
  137:3 127
Proverbs
  14:6 44
  17:7 47
  22:18 47
Ecclesiastes
  5:9 31
  9:5 107
Isaiah
  3:11 79
  3:10–11 78
  12:3 90
  24:23 89
  26:1 67
  32:15 169
  37:24 42
  37:29 42
  37:32 53
  43:18–19 89
  58:6 138
Jeremiah
  2:2–3 166
  29:7 .... 126, 138

183

29:7— 125
29:4-7 127
Daniel
7:26 171
7:27 171
9:7 30
Micah
6:3 29

Habakkuk
3:2 167
Zechariah
4:2 167
4:6 .... 162, 167
6:13 55
8:23 52

Scripture Index

New Testament

Matthew
- 3:15 112
- 5:39 132
- 11:29 24
- 13:33 183
- 16:17 170
- 23:8 68
- 23:23 65
- 26:28 149
- 26:52 .... 131, 133
- 28:19 105
- 28:20 .... 165, 168

Mark
- 12:17 140

Luke
- 3:13 134
- 3:14 135
- 17:10 49
- 17:20–21 181
- 19:10 146
- 24:53 84

John
- 3:16 146
- 8:32 153
- 8:43 146
- 14:6 146
- 14:12 168
- 16:24 90
- 17:17 153
- 18:36 133
- 21:17 86

Acts
- 2:38 112
- 2:42 85
- 2:46 84
- 4:12 147
- 4:36 37
- 5:41 84
- 5:42 48
- 6:4 39
- 6:7 169
- 10:43 146
- 11:21 168
- 11:23 37
- 11:24 .... 35, 37, 52, 54, 57
- 13:52 92
- 14:1 168
- 16:14 169
- 16:25 84
- 16:30 150
- 18:10 169
- 19:2 46
- 19:4 103
- 20:26 79
- 22:16 106

Romans
- 1:1 55
- 1:9 86
- 6:14 151
- 6:17 152
- 6:3–4 107
- 8:15 87
- 8:16 165
- 8:21 64
- 8:26 165
- 10:9 148
- 13:4 134
- 14:17 90

1 Corinthians
- 1:23 147
- 2:2 147
- 3:9 54
- 9:16 78
- 10:12 113

10:1–6 113
12:31 42
13:1–2 39
15:29 112
15:33 155
15:1–3 147

2 Corinthians
1:12 41
2:14 168
4:13 86
5:16 157
6:14–17 71
10:4 169
11:4 152
12:9 55
12:10 55
12:14 55
13:14 114

Galatians
1:9 78
3:1 155
3:26 103
3:28 118
3:24–27 103
4:11 155
4:19 155
4:20 155
5:7 155
5:12 144
5:15 155
5:16 155
5:22 43
5:26 155

Ephesians
3:8 21
3:14–19 21
4:21 146
5:18 43

Philippians
2:7 154
3:14 153

Colossians
2:20 107
3:23 31

1 Thessalonians
4:9 48
5:16 95
5:18 95

2 Thessalonians
2:10 159

1 Timothy
1:11 .... 71, 154
1:15 147
4:15 39

2 Timothy
2:17 151
3:7 50

Titus
1:4 146

Hebrews
3:7–13 156
4:2 50
12:28 173
12:15–16 156
13:9 50
13:17 55

James
1:155
1:2 95
1:9 95
1:18 153
4:2–3 170
5:9 89
5:13–16 170

1 Peter
1:8 84
1:15 154
3:20–21 106
4:7 89

2 Peter
3:12 14

Scripture Index

1 John
  1:151
  2:20 42
  2:23 149
  2:27 44
  4:6 152
  5:1 .... 78, 148
  5:5 148
  5:11 .... 147, 149
  5:12 149
2 John
  9–10 157
  9 157
3 John
  1 157
  4 145

Jude
  3 146
Revelation
  2:2 .... 68, 144
  2:5 .... 28, 30
  3:2 30
  3:2–3 28
  10:7 171
  11:15 172
  12:11 133
  18:19 94
  18:20 94
  19:1–3 94
  22:20 89

www.ingramcontent.com/pod-product-compliance
Lightning Source LLC
Chambersburg PA
CBHW021425070526
44577CB00001B/59